If you find yourself exhausted by the chaos of your thoughts, Hayley Morgan's practical and lovely book, *Preach to Yourself*, will lift your eyes up to heaven to find peace, truth, and clarity from God—the only One who can give it to us.

JENNIE ALLEN, author of *Nothing to Prove* and
founder and visionary of IF:Gathering

You know who I want to preach to me about God, about the Word, about anything? The gal who is already preaching to herself. I'm here to tell you, from a front-row point of view, that Hayley Morgan is a woman who speaks truth to herself—powered by the Holy Spirit and armed with the Word of God. Enjoy this book and embrace this tool that will change your life and strengthen your appetite for our Father.

JESS CONNOLLY, author and speaker

Hayley Morgan's work here is that of a butterfly collector pinning down each fleeting, gossamer lie from our brains and securing it to what holds: an unchanging wall of truth. Like the monarch, may we emerge with patterns anew.

ERIN LOECHNER, author of *Chasing Slow* and
blogger at DesignforMankind.com

There's a voice in my head that tells me I'm not enough. Some days it's quiet, and some days it's super shouty. It's the strangest thing to discover the back of your brain muttering mean things about yourself. The message of *Preach to Yourself* is an antidote—one I urgently believe all women need, lest we die from our self-poisoning. Please act now and open this book.

LISA-JO BAKER, bestselling author of *Never Unfriended* and *Surprised by Motherhood*

When I go to describe this book to other people, I will certainly lead with the word *important*. Hayley Morgan isn't offering anyone a Band-Aid or a quick fix. She has written a manual, in the voice of an old friend, that will keep you practicing for the long haul. This book invites us to practice, to shake off the lies we've long told ourselves, and to wake up to a full life. You don't have to spend your life exhausted and living on empty. *Preach to Yourself* offers a different path—one rooted in grace, truth, and the concrete Word of God. I thank God for truth-tellers like Hayley Morgan.

HANNAH BRENCHER, author of *Come Matter Here*

If you're feeling frustrated or powerless because of negative self-talk, there's good news. Hayley Morgan is a kind guide offering practical and scriptural ways to break away from the bad news loop that cycles through your heart and mind.

SUSIE DAVIS, author of *Unafraid* and cofounder
of Austin Christian Fellowship

PREACH to YOURSELF

PREACH to YOURSELF

When Your Inner Critic Comes Calling, Talk Back with Truth

HAYLEY MORGAN

ZONDERVAN

ZONDERVAN

Preach to Yourself
Copyright © 2018 by Hayley Morgan

Requests for information should be addressed to:
Zondervan, *3900 Sparks Dr. SE, Grand Rapids, Michigan 49546*

ISBN 978-0-310-34577-0 (softcover)

ISBN 978-0-310-35668-4 (audio)

ISBN 978-0-310-34578-7 (ebook)

Published in association with literary agent Jenni Burke of D.C. Jacobson & Associates LLC, an Author Management Company. www.dcjacobson.com.

Cover design: Connie Gabbert Design + Illustration
Interior design: Kait Lamphere

First printing August 2018 / Printed in the United States of America

To Noah, Cooper, Asher, and Eli—
may you learn
to always tell yourself good news.

Here is a trustworthy saying that deserves full acceptance: Christ Jesus came into the world to save sinners—of whom I am the worst. But for that very reason I was shown mercy so that in me, the worst of sinners, Christ Jesus might display his immense patience as an example for those who would believe in him and receive eternal life. Now to the King eternal, immortal, invisible, the only God, be honor and glory for ever and ever. Amen.

1 TIMOTHY 1:15–17

Contents

Part 1:
WHAT IS THE PROBLEM?

Part 2:
WHAT KEEPS US FROM BELIEVING
THE GOOD NEWS?

Part 3:

PREACH TO YOURSELF

Part 4:

WHOLEHEARTED AND
SINGLE-MINDED LIVING

Foreword

---

*H*i, friend!

Every day, I get to look inside women's brains—well, their day planners (essentially the same thing). Each year, I am meticulous as I create our Simplified Planners, because I know that a great tool makes planning your time so much more enjoyable and so much easier. I love making sure the lines are spaced perfectly, the icons are adorable, and the experience is lovely. It's not a shallow pursuit. I squint and measure and plot and painstakingly improve our planners, because I believe in helping women simplify their lives to find greater joy. In growing our brand, Simplified®, I've come to see that the way we spend our days indicates a lot about the condition of our hearts.

I believe there is more to life than overwhelm, and that same belief applies to our minds just as much as to our days. The work I do means I get to be up close and personal with people's plans and hopes and dreams. I get to help them make room for the best things in life.

I believe simple is best. In a world that is busy, noisy, chaotic, and cluttered, I am absolutely positive there is a better way for us to move through our days. I live my life to inspire and empower women to simplify. I know the laundry will not wait. I know the kids will need to be fed—I have three of my own (including twins!). I know there is always a job to be done or some worthy task to complete. But I believe that with a little forward thinking, we can find joy and simplicity in the mess of life and the busyness in our heads.

My work with Simplified means I'm always looking for new and better ways to help women corral and conquer their days. In that same vein, *Preach to Yourself* is a tool for our minds. Just as our days tend to follow natural patterns and rhythms, our minds do the same thing. In our minds, we loop around and around familiar patterns so often that they sound good and true.

"This day is terrible." "I should just give up." "Why am I so inadequate?"

We'd never ever say these things to our best friend. So why do we let our minds run around without the same kind of intention we use to plan our days?

As much as we care for our time, we need to do the same for our minds. It all starts there. I've always felt that by looking at someone's day planner, you could see the stuff that's really important to them. What do they make time for? What is totally missing from their days? I think the same is true about the things we think about. The thoughts that run through our heads all the time show what we *really* believe to be true.

Preach to Yourself gives us a look at what is causing this mental clutter and this voice that's constantly telling us bad news. Hayley looks to the Bible for timeless ways of ordering our minds so that our heads and our hearts line up. It's about the hard but good work of filtering out the mess so we can hear clearly. And as our minds grow to be more like Jesus', we will find it easier and easier to have joy and peace there. It's possible and totally worth it.

Emily Ley, author of the bestselling
Grace, Not Perfection

Prologue

*L*et's kick this off with an honest confession, shall we? It's easy for me to get stuck in my head. That whooshing and whirring, loud and purring brain of mine can feel like the entirety of who I am.

Jesus was a whole human who had a head and a heart and a spirit. I forget that Jesus came to this earth, not as a brain in a Mason jar floating in formaldehyde, but as an embodied, incarnate, integral person. His head and His heart were in perfect alignment to obey His Father. His thoughts lined up with what He believed (*knew* even!) to be true, and His actions followed suit.

Our thoughts are both indicators of deeper issues and can be problems in themselves. It's wise that you're here reading this book. We're going to venture into the middle of ourselves, to the core of who we are. We're going to look at our heads and our hearts; we're going to look at the gap that stands in the middle; and we're going to ask God to close it. We're going to learn to obey with our minds and our hands and our feet so that we're living integrated lives, every part of us lined up to the glory of God.

Our loud minds can be quieted with God's loving-kindness. Our wrongheaded thoughts can be put to death, and we really can live a life dwelling on—incarnating, really—resurrection truth. In order to live in this wholehearted and clearheaded integrity, we need to submit our beliefs and our thoughts to a God who is able to make sense of it all. I have tried, and I am convinced that trying hard is not enough. This kind of life change will require that we partner with a supernatural God.

I need to tell you that we have the opportunity to be living, breathing examples of Jesus walking around in the world. We do! But our flesh is not inclined to want to agree. And our brain, that beautifully complex organ that holds our thoughts, is quite literally flesh! Unreformed by God, we'll go about our days frantic, worried, dour, or fussy. This is not the way of Jesus. This is not a Christlike representation of Him to a hurting world. Neither is this the way you would want to spend this one life you've got.

I am guessing that if you've picked up this book, you know the dichotomy I feel sometimes. What I really believe, on a head level, is not what I actually dwell on in my heart. And because I dwell on other things, what I really believe doesn't make a home in me. It doesn't change me. I want the power of God. I want Him to change me. But I'm walking around like I believe this fuss and frenzy here in front of me is all there is.

Now, this temporal world is *not* all there is. There is a perfect, renewed kingdom of God coming, and there is a foretaste of it here and now. We can almost hear it in the cry of a baby and the consoling words of its mother. We can catch a glimpse of it in the endless lapping of waves on the shore. We can sense it when we give a gift that costs us dearly. There is a deep satisfaction and peace that follow Jesus everywhere, and if you're a believer, His Spirit has come to dwell inside *you*. This is good news!

I'm just reminding you of all these good things so that you can contrast it with the bad news you tell yourself. Do you spend your time telling yourself that nothing's ever going to change? That life is too hard? That it's all just hopeless?

Why when we *know* the good news of Jesus do we repeat to ourselves the bad news of this world? Why when Paul writes that "we have the mind of Christ" (1 Corinthians 2:16) do we desperately hold on to our own bad news loops?

Let's look deeper into the source of the problem, to where things have gone wrong, because then we'll be able to look to God for the answer. It's going to take some brave and steady work on your part, as it has on mine. I have gone before you in this challenge, and I'm still walking beside you. This isn't a one-shot sort of deal. You will learn to embody truth, and that will be a skill you take with you and practice every day until you meet the very One who *is* truth.

PART ONE

What Is the Problem?

CHAPTER ONE

We're Tired of Being Halfhearted and Double-Minded

I obviously need help! I realize that I don't have what it takes. I can will it, but I can't *do* it. I decide to do good, but I don't *really* do it; I decide not to do bad, but then I do it anyway. My decisions, such as they are, don't result in actions. Something has gone wrong deep within me and gets the better of me every time.

PAUL IN ROMANS 7:18–20 (MSG)

It feels delicious, this sleep. It's all mine, with no distractions and no one who needs me at all. No emails to read, no to-dos on my list, and time crawls in that unhurried and blurry way. My mind is silent like I don't experience in the daylight hours. As I rub my eyes, those sleepy liminal moments feel slow and quiet and delightful for someone like me.

I know it won't last long though. From the moment I tip over the side of the bed and plant my feet on the ground, my mind will be busy. It's loud, and it's often not a very companionable friend.

I kick the covers off, breaking out of my warm cocoon, and the cool air presses my mind to attention. I lie there, aware of the day now. As my mind wrestles to awareness, the thoughts are coming, slowly warming up like runners aiming to hit their stride. I know if I lie here too long, my mind will start racing and I'll never catch up with it the whole day long. This is how days get away from me.

I press my toes into the carpet and rise into the day. I have another chance to move through my day in a way I'd like to live—a way "worthy of the gospel of Christ" (Philippians 1:27; see also Ephesians 4:1), worthy of the God I've devoted my whole life to. It sounds heady and noble, but in reality, this service, this devotion, feels frustrating sometimes.

I make my way down the stairs, and I'm aware of stepping over the floorboards I know to be creaky. Those tiny noises have the power to awaken a whole host of sons I share my house with, my life with. I'm alone with my thoughts for now, and it's best that way. I power up the coffee maker, knowing that the jolt of this brew will invite a quickness into thoughts that isn't entirely helpful, but is welcomed.

The thoughts that pepper my consciousness don't match up with what I thought I'd be offering up two decades into my Christian life. I thought I'd have moved on to loftier things. More important heavenly things. But my mind feels particularly human. I know what Scripture spells out. I know what a Christian life could look like, but my mind doesn't seem to reflect what I see in Scripture a lot of the time.

I've believed in, followed, and modeled my whole life after Jesus for what seems like forever, and I still feel like an amateur. I cowrote a book called *Wild and Free*, which is all about living in the wild freedom that God has for us, and I still don't feel like I've mastered the message. And while I know that God and His grace stand every day in that gap, I still feel ashamed sometimes, if I'm honest. The gap between what I know with my head to be true and what I feel in my heart stings. It feels like I should have fully figured it out by now. I should be able to check "Live Wild and Free" off my spiritual to-do list. But instead, I'm still practicing every single day. My head knows that God doesn't call me or anyone to be perfect, and I know that practice is the story of the Christian life. And a beautiful practice at that! Yet I struggle to accept this truth sometimes.

It occurs to me that this gap is where I uncomfortably encounter the dissonance between my head and heart. I feel like I've learned enough to be an expert on "wild and free." I know all the right answers. But my heart still needs a steady reminding. I had already done all the research and know all the right answers.

It isn't that I need to know more or know better. It turns out I need time to sit with the knowledge, boldness to preach it to myself, and discipline to exercise the truth every chance I get.

Of course, isn't that how life is? We never quite arrive in all our years on this old and broken earth. We are in constant need of grace, always cycling along the learning curve.

I sit at the table with my black coffee and sprouted grain toast with almond butter. This has become my routine, my regimen to start the day. And I know that like training myself to eat well, this believing what I know to be true is always going to be a muscle memory/faithfulness kind of thing.

No matter how long we are believers, God is always doing something new. He's always impressing something fresh into our minds and hearts. It's our job to follow Him. I need to train in order to move what I know in my head to be true down to a deep-seated belief in my heart.

I start my day with a basic, solid breakfast because I want to start my day in health. It hasn't always been this way. I'd be delighted with a steady stream of Diet Coke and Snickers, but I know that's not the kind of nutrition my body needs. But I'm training my body for health. And I can do that with my spirit too.

Many women I've met have voiced the same frustration of not being able to embody what they believe. It's like we are wearing the clothes, not becoming the person. Like actors in a really great adventure movie, it's as if we know the script inside out, but we still wish it was real life.

I've found that there is no shortcut or easy answer to this

problem of our lives not lining up completely. Ultimately, small steps of obedience have allowed me to close the gap between what I've learned and read in the Bible and what my head and heart are really doing. I need to make an intentional effort to make these good beliefs part of my actual, everyday life. They cannot live on pages but need to come and make a home in my heart. When I start to bring things out of my pool of knowledge and into my life, I don't just *know*, but I *understand* new, deeper parts of Jesus' hope for us and experience a deeper connectedness with God.

There is a big difference between head knowledge and embodied understanding. The first stays in the brain, while the second unfolds into the real world. It may not seem like it at first, because these words are used pretty much interchangeably, especially in the context of learning. But let's get comfortable with nuance, because nuance helps us see things more fully.

Knowledge is about being aware. It's about comprehending facts and figures. It's retaining what you've read or remembering what you've seen in a movie. Knowledge is the yield of acquiring a certain teaching from someone else. You've received their transmission. Knowledge is being able to repeat what you have received.

But somehow, understanding is different. It seems deeper and more enduring. It's more akin to wisdom. What does it look like when you really get something on a gut level? Does it look different when you've lived and learned a deeply transformational lesson?

Understanding is more about mastery and absorption. It lends a more subjective tone rather than the objective stance of knowledge. It's almost like knowledge is a multiple-choice test and understanding is the essay.

I'm an excellent test taker. Standardized tests were made for the weird way my mind works. Even when I hadn't studied or really mastered the material, I could still score well on a multiple-choice test in my high school and college days. But an essay test is harder to manipulate or complete halfheartedly. An essay test demands a thorough understanding of the material.

My husband, Mike, is always finding insightful videos online, and he found a YouTube account called Smarter Every Day. In this video, an American engineer named Destin Sandlin ruined his ability to do something he had taken for granted since he was six years old. It all started when his friend Barney, a welder, gave him a gift. Wearing Carhartt jackets in a chilly garage, several friends and coworkers gathered to watch it all unfold. They all wondered what would happen.

You see, Barney had fashioned a bike for his buddy Destin. He had welded gears to the body and the bars, meaning that the handlebars, although they looked the same, functioned backward.

The nervous laughter was heady. You could see the steam of their breath as they chuckled and gathered in a circle. Everyone was passing the bike around, swiveling it back and forth as though to do a quick hand-eye coordination test. The men looking on wondered how hard it could be to ride a backward bike. As it turns out—very hard!

Like most of us, Destin knew how to ride a standard bike. He'd learned twenty-five years earlier, in the fading sunlight of an autumn evening. His smile was as bright and wide as the stripe on his 1980s sweatshirt when his six-year-old self finally figured it all out. We all remember that feeling. Instead of wobbling back and forth, something clicks. We find our balance, and then we glide away forever. They say some things are "just like riding a bike"—meaning that you never forget.

Now, intellectually, Destin knew how to ride this backward

bike. Instead of the standard "turn left, go left" and "turn right, go right," it should be the opposite. When he turned the bars to the left, the wheel should go to the right. When he turned the bars to the right, the wheel should go to the left. It's a simple thing to see and know. He could have spouted off in a quick speech how he was planning to ride this crazy backward bike.

It all sounded easy enough, so Destin hopped on the bike before a crowd of cold, but good-humored onlookers. He sat his rear end on the seat and pushed off. Destin didn't last two whole seconds before the tire slid out from under him, causing him to plant his foot on the ground for balance, effectively ending the bike ride before it even got started.

Like a six-year-old, Destin tried again. The second time wasn't even marginally better. Picture it—a grown man getting on a bike confidently and falling off in a matter of seconds. He was giggling like a child, but inside he was embarrassed and frustrated that his mind was not taking the information it knew and transferring it into something his whole self understood.

Now, isn't that something we all want to know? Why can't our brains take something we intellectually know, something that seems easy, and process it into something we just get with our whole selves. We've all experienced the difficulty of putting our head knowledge into life practice. As I was learning about Destin's difficulty with this backward bike, I deeply identified with his frustration. How many times in my life had I been confronted with the fact that I knew what I needed to know but still couldn't make those things happen?

Many people who believe in God get stuck here, finding the rich Christian life out of their grasp. They may hit this point of frustration, but at some point, they relent and settle. One cannot struggle in frustration forever, so they keep God in their heads and tuck away the hope of ever knowing Him in their hearts. They intellectually believe in God, but they do not functionally experience His presence or His goodness in their life.

If we get stuck here, we're giving up before the going gets good. We're settling for less of Jesus—and a diminished Jesus is not the true Jesus at all.

It's not just you or me. There is a dissonance in the life of every believer. I've heard it called an integrity gap or even hypocrisy. In my Christian life, the words *integrity* and *hypocrisy* have felt loaded and burdensome. But this idea of an integrity gap is describing what it's like when our heads and our hearts are not lined up. These may be apt names for the mismatch, but I think it's actually more banal and run-of-the-mill than those words suggest. I'm telling you, *we don't actually believe what we say we believe.* We don't have that bone-deep belief that we want, and it causes us to live halfheartedly, settling for a watered-down, cheap counterfeit of the greatest love story of all time.

This halfhearted acceptance of a religion based on try-hard regulations instead of on embracing the provision of the kind of power it takes to raise a person from the dead is achingly sad. You'd do just as well to be living in the time of Moses when the Law was all they had.

But you live in the twenty-first century, with the benefit of hindsight and a whole book alerting you to the fact that Jesus is alive. You live in a time when Jesus has fulfilled the Law and invites you into a life of grace and righteousness through His very nature. This is fantastic and utterly life-changing news.

Why is there a gap between Sunday certainty and the loop that plays in our heads? Even the most sincere Christian battles this lackluster and defeatist kind of faith. There is a gap between the kind of faith they're experiencing and the truth they profess to believe. The problem is that this gap robs the believer of the abundant life and peace that Christ has for us. It also massively diminishes our testimony, because we're often living joyless, fruitless lives.

- "My head believes that Jesus is real and His death has given me life, so why do I feel so blah about it?"
- "My head believes I am a beloved daughter of God, so why does my heart feel so ashamed?"
- "My head believes that God is my Helper and Provider, so why does my heart feel the anxieties of scarcity?"
- "My head believes that God will direct me, so why does my heart feel so afraid to follow?"

This dissonance is evident in every believer's life to some degree. As followers of Christ, God is constantly sanctifying us and making us more Christlike. So as we grow and mature in our Christian life, the gap between what our heads know and our hearts believe should narrow. However, the here and now is still a reality we must face.

The gap is present from the top down. It's present in our Christian leaders, and it's present in the saints who are barely getting by. This dissonance is a sign that our beliefs are lining up correctly. We may *say* we believe something, and a Christian leader may *say* they believe something, but our actions are really our beliefs with flesh on. Whether an exhausted church girl or a pastor of a church, we all need to make sure this gap between our heads and our hearts doesn't get away from us.

May I ask you a question? How are you? If I was sitting down with you, looking into your eyes, what would you tell me? What does your heart tell you?

I often find that a head-heart gap shows itself through easily recognizable signals.

1. You feel bogged down. You are feeling the weight of the world, and it's heavy! You know you're not supposed to be the one in control, but you feel like it's all on your shoulders. If it's going to get done, it's going to have to be you. The details feel like they're piling up, and it's all so much. You're not sure you'll ever get out from under how you're feeling.

2. You feel chaotic. You can't keep it all straight. It feels like you're being tossed around. You feel like a tiny one-person kayak in the middle of the perfect storm. The tempest is swelling all around you. It feels like a sudden bolt of lightning and a roaring clap of thunder—and your boat is taking on water. You don't know which stressor to fight first. It all feels overwhelming.

3. You feel afraid. You're constantly fearful. You're terrified to make the wrong next move. It feels like the worst thing you can do is fail, and you think it's likely to happen. You are afraid of what people will think and what will happen to your heart if you sink miserably. You're making yourself sick just thinking about how many risks there are in life.

4. You feel unsure. You have no confidence in the Lord's direction. You're waffling. You're on the fence. You don't know the next right move to make, and the only thing you're sure of is that God is going to be mad if you get it wrong. You feel like you might step out of God's will if you make a wrong turn.

5. You feel like you're going around in circles. You're indecisive. You're in a traffic roundabout and stuck there. You don't want to pick a direction and leave the roundabout, so instead of taking action, you just keep returning to the question at hand. You go around and around and around. You analyze everything in eighteen different ways. You think maybe if you give it enough time, God won't let you make a wrong choice.

6. You feel like a phony. You know deep down that something isn't right. You don't feel like a whole person, but kind of like a halfway, watered-down version of yourself. You don't do what you think you should do. You don't feel what you think you should feel. You're terrified that people can see through you. Can people see that you're having a hard time with how living a Christian life goes?

7. You feel powerless. You don't feel the power of God. You feel weak and far from powerful. You wonder if you have any strength left. You're tired of fighting with yourself, weak from fighting for yourself, and exhausted from trying to do the right thing all the time. You're positive that nothing is ever going to change.

8. You feel frustrated. You are annoyed, bitter, and frustrated that nothing you're trying to do to have an abundant life is working. You've set goals; you've made vision boards; you've chased hard after your best life. But you're tired of strong-arming your way into a new life when Jesus promised that His "yoke is easy" and His "burden is light" (Matthew 11:30). Why is it so hard for you when it doesn't seem like it's hard for other people?

9. You feel lackluster. You feel like you're hardly paying attention. You're bored. You feel like the noise of the world is drowning out any hope that God's voice will speak to you. You're feeling dulled by the constant barrage of bad news, both inside your head and on TV. If nothing is ever going to get better, it might be better just to shut down.

10. You feel let down. More than anything, you're disappointed. This isn't what you thought being a Christian was going to be like. It feels like you were sold a false bill of goods, and none of this is what you wanted. Instead of seeing your life changed, it's more of the same—only now you have an extra helping of guilt because of the Jesus thing.

This disconnect has been around for as long as we've had a disconnect with God. In fact, I trace it all the way back to the fall of humanity in Eden. When Adam and Eve first sinned in the garden (Genesis 3:1–7), they experienced dissonance for the first time in human history. I want us to look carefully here, because I believe that Genesis 3 has a lot to teach us about our own affliction of dissonance.

There is great hope in knowing where it all started, because we have a God who has already made a way. He has already conquered this particular human affliction and has provided a way for us to move forward and become whole. Let's first go back to the beginning and read all of Genesis 3 together—don't skip over this part; it's important.

> Now the serpent was more crafty than any of the wild animals the Lord God had made. He said to the woman, "Did God really say, 'You must not eat from any tree in the garden'?"

Satan plants the seed of a lie that God is holding out on us.

> The woman said to the serpent, "We may eat fruit from the trees in the garden, but God did say, 'You must not eat

fruit from the tree that is in the middle of the garden, and you must not touch it, or you will die.'"

Eve tries to talk back to Satan, telling him the truth of what God said. She doesn't make a value judgment here—whether His commands are good or bad. She simply states the command as God told it (with added commands He didn't give—about touching, for example). God essentially said, "There's tons of fruit here and you can have it all, but don't eat from this tree because that fruit isn't good for you. It will cause you harm."

"You will not certainly die," the serpent said to the woman. "For God knows that when you eat from it your eyes will be opened, and you will be like God, knowing good and evil."

The serpent pushes forward here, accusing God of keeping something interesting, important, and powerful from Adam and Eve. Don't we all fear this sometimes? Aren't we tempted to believe that if we don't act now, we're going to miss out? The same accuser in this garden story is the accuser of God and man today. Satan is still out to get us, still out to pit us against God.

When the woman saw that the fruit of the tree was good for food and pleasing to the eye, and also desirable for gaining wisdom, she took some and ate it. She also gave some to her husband, who was with her, and he ate it.

Eve decided that the fruit looked mighty delicious, and she wanted to know everything God knew. So she chomped down on that fruit and shared a bite with her husband. She knew better, and she did it anyway. How often are we like Eve? We know, but we don't understand.

Then the eyes of both of them were opened, and they realized they were naked; so they sewed fig leaves together and made coverings for themselves.

Adam and Eve didn't know nakedness or shame before that apple, but now they felt the air on their nude bodies and felt vulnerable. Why did they feel less at home in the garden now that they were supposed to be more like God?

Then the man and his wife heard the sound of the Lord God as he was walking in the garden in the cool of the day, and they hid from the Lord God among the trees of the garden. But the Lord God called to the man, "Where are you?"

God knew where Adam and Eve were, but the perfect harmony between them had been severed. He asked them where they were in order to make it clear that all could no longer be as it had been.

He answered, "I heard you in the garden, and I was afraid because I was naked; so I hid."

But Adam already knew this. Adam knew he was hiding from God. We all hide from God when we're afraid to be seen as we are. When we fall short of expectation, we want to shine up, cover up, or split up. We want to make ourselves look better, hide, or cut off the relationship all together.

> And he said, "Who told you that you were naked? Have you eaten from the tree that I commanded you not to eat from?"

God knows, but He's always going to ask us anyway. Admitting what we've done is part of repenting. We cannot be forgiven of what we don't own up to.

> The man said, "The woman you put here with me—she gave me some fruit from the tree, and I ate it."

Adam blames Eve. But he admits that he ate the fruit. This is the dissonance now existing between each other.

> Then the Lord God said to the woman, "What is this you have done?"
> The woman said, "The serpent deceived me, and I ate."

Now God comes to Eve and asks her to own up to what she's done. Eve blames Satan, but admits that she ate the fruit.

> So the Lord God said to the serpent, "Because you have done this,
>
> > "Cursed are you above all livestock
> >   and all wild animals!
> > You will crawl on your belly

> and you will eat dust
>> all the days of your life.
> And I will put enmity
>> between you and the woman,
>> and between your offspring and hers;
> he will crush your head,
>> and you will strike his heel."

This is the curse on Satan. That serpent is going to eat dust forever, and eventually God says that Eve's offspring will crush him underfoot.

> To the woman he said,

> "I will make your pains in childbearing very severe;
>> with painful labor you will give birth to children.
> Your desire will be for your husband,
>> and he will rule over you."

Giving life was going to be excruciating for the woman. It was going to take labor—hard work—for it to come to pass. The next part is harder to understand, because one would think a woman desiring her husband would be a good thing. The easiest way to explain this verse is that it's marking that Adam and Eve (and therefore humankind) will be in conflict with one another from here on out. The NLT translates v. 16b as such: "And you will desire to control your husband, but he will rule over you." The words "he will rule over you" are not a biblical command, but a reality of what will happen because of the fall.

To Adam he said, "Because you listened to your wife and ate fruit from the tree about which I commanded you, 'You must not eat from it,'

> "Cursed is the ground because of you;
>> through painful toil you will eat food from it
>> all the days of your life.
> It will produce thorns and thistles for you,
>> and you will eat the plants of the field.
> By the sweat of your brow
>> you will eat your food
> until you return to the ground,
>> since from it you were taken;
> for dust you are
>> and to dust you will return."

God also broke the happy agreement between Adam and the earth. The earth previously grew anything Adam and Eve needed. Now Adam was going to have to work against the cursed ground and work for his food. The ground that produced life-giving food was also going to produce thorns and thistles.

Adam named his wife Eve, because she would become the mother of all the living.

The Lord God made garments of skin for Adam and his wife and clothed them.

God shows His mercy to Adam and Eve and covers their shame.

> And the LORD God said, "The man has now become like one of us, knowing good and evil. He must not be allowed to reach out his hand and take also from the tree of life and eat, and live forever."

Being kicked out of the garden is also a mercy. Our death will keep us from living forever in this fallen state. After we die, if we are believers in and followers of Jesus, we will be made completely new and be in perfect communion with God again.

> So the LORD God banished him from the Garden of Eden to work the ground from which he had been taken. After he drove the man out, he placed on the east side of the Garden of Eden cherubim and a flaming sword flashing back and forth to guard the way to the tree of life.

This dissonance is a curse of the fall. It is a condition of our humanity, part of our fallen nature. We aren't lined up perfectly with God, because the only way to do that is through Jesus.

It's not only with God that we suffer misalignment, but we're also not in sync with ourselves or with others.

DISSONANCE WITH GOD

In the Garden of Eden, God and Adam and Eve walked together in uncompromised communion. When you hear "the cool of the day" in Genesis 3:8, the garden seems like a really lovely place to be. I imagine it to be that kind of refreshing, dewy cool of the morning. I imagine the garden being a wild place rather than a tamed, cultivated garden. I imagine Adam and Eve squishing down tall grass as they walked. They were living in absolutely unsullied connection with God, so why did they so easily believe the lie that God was holding out on them? Why did they begin to feel like they wanted to hide from Him?

Our dissonance with God shows itself in many ways:

- We believe He created us, but that He's disinterested or not intimately involved now.
- We don't believe He's good, because we're afraid of Him.
- We believe He forgave us once, but now it's up to us.
- We feel like He's constantly rolling His eyes at us.
- We believe He likes (and blesses) some people more than us.
- We believe God is holding out on us (like Eve believed in the garden).
- We believe He's more interested in what we do for Him than in who we are in Him.

DISSONANCE WITHIN OURSELVES

We're out of whack with ourselves. Adam and Even felt shame in their nakedness after their sin. They didn't even know what nakedness was before the fall, but afterward they couldn't stop thinking about it. Inherent in the story of the fall of Adam and Eve is that confusion entered the mix. They were still going to have food, but there would now be thistles and thorns growing with the good plants. They'd have to labor through the bad to get to the good, and they'd have to discern which was which. This is a consequence of having the knowledge of good and evil. You have to decide between the two—what is good and what is evil? What was meant for their good, now that they had eaten from the tree of knowledge of good and evil, became confusing and muddied.

Here are some examples of the dissonance we feel with our-selves:

- We believe we're worse than other people.
- We believe we're victims of other people.
- We believe we'll get it right next time.
- We believe we can do it on our own.
- We feel shame, fear, frustration, and despair all the time.
- We believe ourselves to be as wise as God (like Eve in the garden).

DISSONANCE WITH OTHERS

Prior to Genesis 3:10, Adam had only ever talked about himself and Eve in the plural term "we." They were one. But after he ate that tempting, shiny apple Adam used the pronoun "I" for the first time. Adam felt like his helper had hurt him. The one he was supposed to be able to trust had led him into temptation. And now, Adam was motivated by his own self-interests, his own self-protection, which means he and Eve were pitted against each other. We experience this break in relationships across the board today. It is exponentially more difficult to have unity than disagreement.

We have come to believe these things about other people:

- They exist for our use.
- They're out to get us.
- They're less than us.
- They're not safe.

This is the world we were born into, and this is our spiritual DNA until we are renewed by Jesus. This is our flesh and what we battle in the world. This dissonance that we feel, the misalignment within ourselves, should not surprise us. It should not make us feel alone or like a misfit. This is the norm, even in the Christian life, but God has given us a way to bear up under the burden and to have victory, to be changed, to be made more like Him.

We need to get to the root of the issue—a root that lies in the way we were created. Our minds were made for complex connection making. It's at the base of our humanity. When used for good, for its intentional purpose, the way our minds make connections is godly and fosters a deep dependency on the Lord. I don't want us to miss the good ways we were created.

But in our humanness, in our less-than-Eden world, our minds can play tricks on us. They can become glitchy and frustrate us. If you're anything like me, I know your mind isn't quiet and well-behaved all the time. So let's dive deep into the words we hear over and over, so we can begin to preach to ourselves the good news instead.

CHAPTER TWO

The Bad News Is on Repeat

Have you realized that most of your unhappiness in life is due to the fact that you are listening to yourself instead of talking to yourself? Take those thoughts that come to you the moment you wake up in the morning. You have not originated them, but they start talking to you, they bring back the problems of yesterday, etc. Somebody is talking . . . Your self is talking to you. Now this man's treatment [in Psalm 42] was this: instead of allowing this self to talk to him, he starts talking to himself. "Why art thou cast down, O my soul?" he asks. His soul had been depressing him, crushing him. So he stands up and says, "Self, listen for a moment, I will speak to you."

MARTYN LLOYD-JONES,
SPIRITUAL DEPRESSION

I've been thinking a lot lately about the idea of the stories we tell ourselves. My mind is never, ever quiet. I was starting to feel limited by the stories my mind was telling me. For some reason, I was my own worst enemy. I had long felt like I was not enough, even when I knew better, and my inner monologue was backing up this belief.

My first thought upon waking and realizing life was going to require energy from me *again* was, *I can't do this.*

My mind chatters all throughout breakfast with Noah, Cooper, Asher, and Eli, thinking, *I'll never be a good enough mom for all these boys.*

At the end of the day as I pull the covers up to my chin, I think back on a day full of failures and few measurable victories and wonder if anything will ever change.

It seemed I wasn't living in the power that God promises, and I couldn't exactly pinpoint why. But I had an idea that the loops playing in my head were not helping the matter.

I suspected I was not the only one with this problem of a loud and bossy mind. One day, I hopped on my computer and dashed off a quick Google Forms survey with the question, "What kind of bad news do you tell yourself every day?" I am not a research scientist, and I almost always believe *done* is better than *perfect*, so I called it "good enough" and sent the survey to my contact list and followers on social media.

Immediately, I started receiving answers. It was as if women had been waiting around to tell someone all the junk rattling around in their minds. As I pored over the answers to the survey, my own mind pinged around, quickly identifying patterns. I kept scrolling, cell by cell by cell on this long spreadsheet. I barely paused, because if I lingered too long, the weight of the answers threatened to sink me. I had been tallying the responses as they came in, and after all was said and done, nearly five hundred women had taken the time to answer my question.

By midnight that same day, I had already collected hundreds of replies. It was obvious that women were eager to off-load the mess that was invading their thoughts. I don't blame them. It's a heavy burden to carry when you really stop to think about what you're ruminating on. My own mind pings around like an over-caffeinated, frenetic pinball machine most days, and I don't want anyone to watch the way the ball moves. I bounce my way through the day, and the thoughts I have aren't always welcome.

I've come to believe that this is how most of us spend our days. Instead of having ordered and disciplined minds, we've become accustomed to the high-paced back-and-forth. We're used to arguing with ourselves amid our own mental civil war. This is not what we want, but this is what we do.

As the apostle Paul writes in Romans 7:18–20 (MSG), "I obviously need help! I realize that I don't have what it takes. I can will it, but I can't *do* it. I decide to do good, but I don't *really* do it; I decide not to do bad, but then I do it anyway. My decisions, such as they are, don't result in actions. Something has gone wrong deep within me and gets the better of me every time."

On Sunday, we go to church; we worship; we connect with other believers. We hear the good news preached—that Jesus died for us and that He's still at work in the world today. We most likely believe this good news *most completely* during these ninety minutes every week.

If our minds kept repeating the truth we heard on Sundays, our inner monologue should sound something like this: "I'm beloved! I've been saved for great things! This world is not my home, and that's okay! I have a family of faith who loves me! I belong in the family of God! My hope is assured!"

However, when we walk out the church doors, what we repeat to ourselves can quickly change. The other six days of the week, we can be tempted to allow our minds to run on a loop of bad beliefs.

I started to call this pattern "The Loop," because that's what it feels like. It's like my mind is a hamster wheel that just keeps spinning. It's the scroll that never ends. I never even questioned it, because these bad beliefs just looked like the landscape inside my head. It's very hard to disbelieve what you hear over and over in your own voice every day. This experience just starts to feel like reality.

These bad beliefs aren't necessarily big, earth-shattering sinful patterns. I'm not talking about debilitating lust or frighteningly violent anger (although there is freedom in Jesus in those things too!). I'm talking about the banal, run-of-the-mill antigospel you probably hear so often in your head and that sounds so much like your own voice that you don't even register it as bad news.

I spent weeks combing through the results of the survey about the bad news we tell ourselves. I read every single answer. With almost a thousand versions of bad news, I found that, with few outliers, they all fell within three main buckets.

These are some of the word-for-word responses I received when I asked the question, "What kind of bad news do you tell yourself every day?"

I can't do this. This is a question of capacity and ability. Do I have what it takes? Will I make it through?

- I'm a failure.
- Am I sure I can do this?
- I'm never going to succeed.
- If I can't handle everything I've taken on, I'm unworthy.
- I'm immature and will never keep up with those around me.
- I'm not cut out for motherhood.
- I'm not smart enough.
- I won't make ends meet.
- I'm too tired.
- This is too hard.
- I'm so bad at this.
- I can't handle this.
- I'll never find time to get this done.

I'm not enough. This loop speaks to the question of identity and worth. Who assigns the value to my life? Is it something that is earned, or is it something that is given? What happens when I don't measure up?

- I'm a mess.
- There's something wrong with me.
- I'm not cool enough for that.
- I am just not measuring up.
- I'm not pretty or skinny enough.
- I'm too quiet and don't talk enough.
- No one likes me.
- I don't make a difference.

- I'm not interesting.
- Others have it easier because they are "blessed."
- I disappoint everyone.
- I am so weak.
- I'm not patient enough.

Nothing is ever going to change. This is a question of futility. Does any of this even matter, and is there hope? I look for words like *never*, *ever*, and *always* in this loop.

- I will always struggle.
- I will never change.
- This is never going to get better.
- I will never get married.
- I will always be gripped by anxiety.
- I'll never accomplish my goals.
- My life will never look the way I want it to.
- I'll never lose the weight.
- This will never get any easier.
- My dream will never happen.
- Will I be alone forever?
- God can't use me.
- I'm done. I give up.
- Why do I even try?

We aren't static creatures. Our minds don't exist in a vacuum apart from the rest of our being. When we believe a lie, we either stuff it down or rev ourselves up to prove it wrong.

If you believe you're not enough, you may stuff it down and drown it out with Netflix, thoughtless shopping, or constant social positioning. You may try to cheer yourself up and forget you ever thought such a thing. You may just say, "I'm great. I'm fine. Life is good. #TooBlessedToBeStressed."

If you believe that nothing is ever going to change, you may go into hyperdrive trying to prove yourself wrong. You may become like Wonder Woman with all your planning, dreaming, goal setting, and executing in the hopes that someday life will be different.

These behaviors are coping mechanisms, and they're two sides of the same coin. The problem with a coping mechanism is that it functions more like a Band-Aid than a cure-all. Coping mechanisms are meant for short-term "getting through." They're part of your emotional repertoire, the tools you've had since you were born. They helped you feel safe when you were a child and had no power for yourself.

But you don't need to only cope anymore. You are an adult, held by the Creator of the lowly ant and the mighty oak, loved by the God who doesn't let even a sparrow fall from the sky without His say. It's time to focus on what's going on in your thoughts so you can begin to put a stop to the noise in your head.

These are some of the responses to my survey question, "How do these thoughts affect your days?"

- They make them full of anxiety and unneeded pressure.
- They make me sad.
- They make me second-guess my decisions.
- They stop me from trying.
- My days feel heavy and unjoyful.
- They weigh me down and hold me back.
- I find myself tense and stressed all the time.

- It's essentially learned helplessness—this is the way things are, and it will always be this way.
- They sound real—they sound like truth—so they keep me in a funk, not trusting the people or relationships around me.
- They deter me from stepping out or living loved.
- They make me want to be lazy and just not try.
- They keep me focused on the past or the future, not the present. They make me feel bad about myself.
- These thoughts make me feel tired, down, and weak.
- They feel isolating, particularly from family.
- I waste my time thinking how I should have and could have done or said things differently.
- They take a toll on my confidence and cause me to stumble.
- These lies are the framework for everything.
- I feel anxious—overthinking, worrying, and paralyzed by the thought of making a wrong move.
- They weigh heavily and rob so much of the freedom the Lord has created me for—now freedom seems so impossible, and it's easier to stay in the bondage.
- It's difficult to see or feel light when my mind is fixed on these dark or heavy thoughts.
- I think they impact my days more than I even know—by how I view myself, how I interact with friends, how I view my job, how I think God sees me, and how I view God.
- I'm exhausted. I need a nap just from mental battles.
- They place too much pressure on my performance.
- They make me want to give up.

I'm the kind of girl who likes silence in the car. With four children, the only silence I get is when I'm alone. You can normally find me pondering lists like the one you just read. I'm always trying to find connections between ideas and information—and silence is the best ingredient for connection making.

One particular day, though, I had what NPR calls a "driveway moment." That summer day felt breezy and hopeful, and I was listening to *This American Life*. I got to the end of my drive home, parked in the driveway, and sat for twenty minutes enthralled by an episode called "The Devil in Me." Nancy Updike, a producer on the show, had asked around to see if people ever felt like they were being influenced by an inner voice that gave them impulses and thoughts they'd like to not have. These people were battling a voice inside themselves that sounded an awful lot like their own voice. It was keeping them in patterns of unwanted behaviors.

The moderator Ira Glass remarked that people had a lot to say when asked about the idea that they are compelled by a voice inside their head—"it was like people had been waiting all their lives for somebody to ask them this question"[1]—and that mirrors my experience with my loops survey. When I asked about the false beliefs that people held and heard all the time in their heads, it seemed like the respondents had been waiting for someone to ask.

This voice people are dying to expose is their inner critic. I believe we all have one. What I call the "inner critic" can also be called your "inner monologue" or "self-talk." Our self-talk illuminates what we believe to be true about ourselves. It is hypothesized that our self-talk is developed by messages we heard in our childhood, by our experiences, and by our takeaways from those experiences. Our inner critic can also be developed by what we observed in others—the things that went well and elicited praise and the things that fell short and elicited criticism.

The inner critic often sounds just like our own voice, but it's negative, condemning, and condescending. We often experience this voice, even though it is silent and internal, as though we are being audibly spoken to.

The things our inner critic tells us may seem all over the place. However, it's fair to say that our inner critic is actually fairly consistent in its message. If we spend the time to look for them and ask God to identify them, the patterns of our inner critic will show us our "core beliefs." Seth Gillihan, a professor of psychology, wrote in *Psychology Today*:

> Core beliefs can be hard to change because they've generally been with us for a long time, and we assume that they're true. Perhaps the biggest obstacle to changing our core beliefs is that *they are strongly self-perpetuating*. When we have a fundamentally negative view of ourselves, we're biased to interpret negative outcomes as evidence of our shortcomings.[2]

NPR's Nancy Updike got an earful when she asked people about what their inner critic sounded like or communicated to them. Here are some of the answers:

- MAN: The voice is irresistible, always. I'm in the thrall of that voice.
- WOMAN: Totally out of control. It's got this life of its own, and I can't tame it anymore.
- MAN: I remember somehow realizing just how finely calibrated the voice was to every nuance, every part of my feelings, including the feeling that I didn't want to smoke

cigarettes. And it's just like, *Might as well have another ciga-rette, because this is it.*

- MAN: The voice definitely brings in also an element of shame. It says, you want everyone to think that you have money. You want everyone to see that you're generous and you can give and put yourself out there financially. It will prove that you're not a poor kid.
- WOMAN: And it also says a lot of mean things too. Your husband's too good for you, you may as well have a glass of wine because without it you won't be as entertaining.
- WOMAN: You better try your hardest to make sure he doesn't take [the ring] away, because he's going to find out the truth about you and how much you suck. So you better distract him with a really thin body.[3]

We all have these inner conversations going on all the time. Yours may sound a little different, depending on your life circumstances. At some point, we've all had this drone of bad news playing out in our minds. But as believers, we know the best news in the world. Why do we struggle to stay anchored in Christ? I am constantly wrestling with this question. I have come to the conclusion that there must be some benefit to us as believers to struggle in this way, or else God could have eliminated it from our life at the point of conversion.

I believe we have a choice right here and right now to see this wrestling as a *good thing*—as something allowed so that we'll prosper. Let me try to convince you. This struggle will push you toward truth more than any other I've known. You'll have to do work that is tedious and exacting. You'll be forced to go over the same ground again and again. It is in this learning and relearning that we see God. We see Him change us, and we yield to His will.

So while we examine the reasons we fall for this liar of an inner voice, let's hold on to hope that this is the good stuff of the faith, that this struggle is a gift, because it deepens our faith from knowing to understanding. We not only intellectually get the truth, but we deep down in our bones *believe* the truth.

Before we can begin to have our hearts changed, though, we need to understand how our brains were made and how our minds work in the first place.

CHAPTER THREE

A Look inside Our Heads

The surface of the earth is soft and impressible by the feet of men; and so with the paths which the mind travels.
HENRY DAVID THOREAU, *WALDEN*

*L*ast winter, in my best attempt at *hygge*, I cozied in with a stack of books. But before I could get too far, I developed a macabre fascination with the recent history of the inexact science of lobotomies. I read a book called *Patient H.M.*,[1] and as these things do, it sent me down a warped rabbit trail on the internet. It turns out that in the mid-twentieth century, there was an exploding field of psychosurgery—the discipline of brain surgery for the purpose of psychiatric relief. I saw photos of women and young boys staring blankly into the camera with vacant black-and-blue eyes.

They'd had lobotomies. The Oxford Dictionary defines a lobotomy as "a surgical operation involving incision into the prefrontal lobe of the brain, formerly used to treat mental illness."[2] It was controversial from the outset, and it was experimental and imprecise in nature. Being disproportionately used on women and children, the procedure was often exploitative—with family members looking for relief for or from their loved ones, and doctors being all too excited to have the opportunity to cut into and research the brain. It seemed like such a barbaric treatment for a condition shown to be mostly treatable in our modern era.

The book followed a man identified only as Patient H.M. He's famous in medical literature, and his real name—Henry Molaison—wasn't released until after his death. He had increasingly debilitating and eventually intractable seizures that stemmed from a bike accident when he was seven years old. Twenty years later, he and his desperate family had heard there may be a surgical solution. Lobotomies had been found to have the strange effect of remedying seizures, and so Henry underwent surgery on September 1, 1953.

The surgery was a success in that it eliminated Henry's seizures. However, because the surgery eliminated his hippocampus and the areas around it, Henry was left unable to remember dating back to about two years before the surgery and was unable to ever make new meaningful memories again. He could learn new motor skills, because his working and procedural memory were intact, but he could not, for all intents and purposes, add to his long-term, explicit memory.

The book's author, Luke Dittrich, told Ed Yong, the writer of an article about Patient H.M., "Henry ended on that operating table. Even the memories from before the operation were experienced by Henry in a very different way than we experience our past. He wasn't able to build a narrative with a beginning middle and end. We're a storytelling species and one of the things taken from Henry was his story."[3]

What surprised me more than anything, though, was how little that doctors and researchers knew about the brain in the not very distant past. The brain was a vast uncharted and undiscovered mystery. It was clear that the brain was responsible for the higher-level functions of a person, but it was unclear just how it all worked.

In the United States, lobotomies began in the early 1940s and ceased almost entirely by the mid-1950s, when antipsychotic medications became available. It was a short-lived, brutal foray into attempts to affect the outcome of a person's thoughts. Once less drastic measures were invented, surgeons no longer needed to destroy entire parts of someone's brain. However questionable the ethics, as is usually the case in early medical advancements, invaluable information was gained from the pursuit of understanding.

And this duality mirrors the reality of the brain. On the one hand, it's an organ like a kidney. It has a function that keeps a person alive. On the other hand, the brain holds deep mystery because it powers our personalities, our actions, and our intentions. It has always been a categorically complex organ that is boundlessly more intricate and integral than it appears at first glance. Authors Gregory Boyd and Al Larson write the following:

> The average adult brain consists of more than 10 billion neurons communicating with one another through more than 10 trillion synaptic connections. (Synaptic connections are the junctions or gaps between the axon and the dendrite of a neuron.) As unbelievable as it sounds, the number of possible neuronal connections in the brain is more than all of the stars in the known universe (approximately 50 billion galaxies with an average of 100 billion stars each). Although the average dendrite is a fraction of a millimeter in size, if you were to line up all the dendrites in your brain, the line would circle the globe five times![4]

Here are a few other fascinating facts:

- Your brain uses 20 percent of your body's energy supply.[5]
- Your neurons send messages at the speed of up to 250 miles per hour.[6]

- If you stretched out all the blood vessels in your brain
  end to end, they'd reach halfway to the moon, measuring
  approximately 120,000 miles.[7]

My grandpa and I have always had this joke that the creases on the surface of the brain each denote a memory made. So when we have a challenging or funny experience together, we always tell each other, with a twinkle in our eye, that we've just made another crease. If only it were that simple!

Our brains are magnificent creations that allow us to act as individuals, made by but apart from God. We are sentient, willful, and able because of the inner workings of our brains.

The internationally recognized educator and expert on mindfulness Daniel Siegel helps us better understand the development of the brain in his book *The Mindful Brain*.[8] Siegel tells us that when we're growing in our mother's belly, our entire nervous system starts out as something called the "ectoderm"—a flat sheet of cells that will eventually become our skin. Then that flat sheet folds together to make up what is called the neural tube—which happens before our mom even missed a period.

The brain will eventually form at one end of the neural tube, and the spinal cord becomes the remainder of the neural tube. We must remember that the nervous system spans far more than just our brain and is actually extended through our body.

When we're developing in the womb, our nervous system sets up its whole infrastructure, its "basic scaffolding." Genetics play a massive role in determining how our neurons will move and attach to each other. As a baby nears full term, the connections between neurons begin to be "influenced by experience."[9]

When we have an "experience," our nervous system activates

"neural firing in response to a stimulus." So experiences cause our neurons to activate, and when neurons activate, "their connections to each other grow and supportive cells and vasculature proliferate."[10]

Our brains end up being about the size of a head of broccoli and account for about one-fiftieth of our body mass. Siegel writes, "One hundred billion neurons are, on average linked to each other via 10,000 synaptic connections, which are created by genes and sculpted by experience: Nature needs nurture. These two important dimensions of human development and neural function are not in opposition."[11]

He goes on to say that "*neuroplasticity* is the term used when connections change in response to experience." Earlier in his book, Siegel wrote, "How we focus attention helps directly shape the mind."[12] Simply put, we can actually *change our mind*.

These changes in our brain alter not only the way our brain is shaped on a micro level; neuroplastic alterations can also change our brain function, our feelings and emotions, and our responses to stress.

What struck me about the lobotomies was the fact that the brain had been unmapped before the psychosurgeons began to do surgery on patients who were awake and aware. Because all previous brain dissections had been done after a patient was dead, there had been no concrete way to figure out what part of the brain was responsible for what function. What area was responsible for allowing us to taste our favorite comfort food? What part of the brain developed a taste for classical music or hip-hop? What section governs our emotions and our attachments to certain things?

There was no way to know until the primitive and controversial surgery of lobotomies came on the medical scene. Because it was psychosurgery, the doctors were attempting to lessen or dull certain behaviors or emotions to make the life of a patient (or sometimes, questionably, the life of the caregiver) easier. In the operating room, the surgeons would make an incision and then ask the patient to perform intellectual or physical tasks. When the surgeons could quiet those particular behaviors, they knew they were working in an area of the brain that governed those tasks.

When I cozied up on my couch, wrapped up in this morbid curiosity with lobotomies and the brain, I couldn't believe how recently researchers were in the dark about the functions of the brain. It truly is a fascinatingly complex organ, and modern-day researchers are only beginning to unfurl the exciting truths held inside.

Thinking of the brain being previously unmapped reminded me of the word *deep* in Scripture. The brain was vast and unknown. *Tehôm*—a Hebrew word, from a root signifying "confusion" or "disturbance"—is poetically applied to the ocean, as in Psalm 42:7 ("deep") because of the restless motion of its waves, but it is used here to describe the chaos as a surging mass of shapeless matter.[13]

The depth is something that hasn't yet been brought under the control of Christ. And this can be said about our minds before they are made like Christ's. They are vast, and they can be noisy. They are dark and unknown.

Imagine that as the psalmist writes Psalm 42, he is near the head of the Jordan River.[14] The Jordan is probably swollen and rushing, with water swirling around and between rocks that jut out of the surface of the water. It is treacherous, to say the least. Psalm 42:7 reads, "Deep calls to deep"—the swirling and confusion just keep coming, one wave after another.

This Scripture illustrates how a mind untethered to Christ can feel. It is tossed in opposing directions. It is chaotic. It is not formed to the likeness of Jesus.

I have felt that unbridled chaos before. The chaos is the everyday difficulty of pursuing a quiet and content mind, one that speaks life and truth over my days. But we have the hope of Jesus. We have the hope of a God who can change things. He knows the intricacies of our minds and how quickly they can get away from us, because He created us to be so profoundly complex.

This complexity is not a surprise to Him. Simple inventions are only capable of simple tasks, but complex inventions are capable of infinitely more. That is the comfort I have as I think of this knowledge of the brain. God created us this way on purpose, and His loving design will allow us to have very complex inner lives that are calmed and governed by His truth and power. We have so much to look forward to!

PART TWO

What keeps Us from Believing the Good News?

CHAPTER FOUR

Our World Is So Noisy

Life today in America is based on the premise of ever-widening circles of contact and communication . . . My mind reels with it. What a circus act we women perform every day of our lives. It puts the trapeze artist to shame. Look at us. We run a tight rope daily, balancing a pile of books on the head. Baby-carriage, parasol, kitchen chair, still under control. Steady now!

This is not the life of simplicity but the life of multiplicity that the wise men warn us of. It leads not to unification but to fragmentation. It does not bring grace; it destroys the soul.

ANNE MORROW LINDBERGH,
A GIFT FROM THE SEA

I've never been accused of having too little going on. I keep a lot of balls in the air, have a lot of chicks in my nest, and spin a lot of plates. All of the typical metaphors for being busy apply to my life—in spades.

Today is a typical Tuesday. Once I got all my big boys on the bus, I drove my littlest son to preschool. He stays there until noon, when my friend and Eli's nanny, Barb, picks him up for some quality time. From 9:30 a.m.—when I get to the office with a coffee and two Diet Cokes in hand—until about noon, I'm working on shipping packages, writing notes to our customers, and ordering product for Nellie Taft, the Made in the USA boutique I own. At noon, my office manager, Lexi, leaves, and I start doing my writing and ministry tasks. I need a lot of quiet to do those tasks, so I work best when I'm alone. And it has to be completely quiet for me to hear what the Lord is leading me to write or say.

At 3 p.m., I leave my quiet cocoon of the empty office to head home to the din of a house of four boys. It's always noisy and always chaotic, and the bouncing of a ball is in the background of every conversation. The noise follows me everywhere unless I purposely shut it down.

When I have other people in the office, I'm drawn to the conversations they're having rather than the one I need to be dictating to the page. If there is music playing, I'm nodding my head and singing along without even realizing it. When I don't make time to get alone and in the quiet, I can't distinguish what's important, because everything loud and urgent rises to the top. It overwhelms me with its intensity. This sense of being overwhelmed is indicative of my work life, but it occurs in my spiritual life as well.

Our culture is a culture of more. We have more computing power. We have more access to people. We have more information than ever before. The average worker says they feel like they work more hours than anyone ever (yet the research indicates the opposite is true).

Why in the world can we not shut these loops off? Why do they keep spinning around on repeat? The problem is that we have to get very quiet to deal with that bully for good. And we're just not willing to be quiet.

When it is quiet, we hear these loops in our heads a little louder. The silence that should bring us peace instead can bring us a nightmare of unmet expectations, frustrated faith, and exhaustion. So instead of submitting to the silence, we bring in the noise. And there is no shortage of noise these days.

There is not enough quietness, stillness, and boredom. It's not that stillness and solitude aren't available, but we don't choose them. We prefer the rowdiness of group texts, the dopamine hit of a favorite Tweet, and the never-ending scroll. We line our calendars with commitment after commitment, believing that if we're busy, we may feel more important.

We believe the American propaganda that we should be

productive and efficient at all times, and if we can just master one elusive life hack, everything will come together.

We don't need to be more productive; what we need to do is cut it out. We need to bring down the volume. This noise isn't benign. It's not simply on in the background like the television while your mom is doing dishes. It all adds up.

Let's take a look at how the noise affects us.

POTENTIAL BUILDS PRESSURE

My whole life, I've been told I could do anything I set my mind to. I am one of the very oldest millennials, and my parents were hot out of the gate to make sure I knew just how special I was. I was wearing pigtails and patent leather Mary Janes when my dad told me I could be the first female president—and in 2020, I will just be old enough to run. There's still a chance!

My dad did presidential flash cards with me, and I memorized in order every president from George Washington to James K. Polk to Jimmy Carter to William Jefferson Clinton. He regaled me with stories of space exploration, and he and my mom took me to space shuttle launches and to gifted and talented programs at the university ninety minutes from my house every Saturday.

I felt empowered by their encouragement and belief, and I also felt like the possibility was a lot to shoulder. How do you ever know you've succeeded if the actual sky doesn't even limit you?

I've toyed with this idea for a long time. It feels sacrosanct to even say in our modern American society, but here goes: I think the ideal of potential is driving us crazy. We believe we can be anything and achieve anything, and we're hungry for it.

Every time I was told, "You have so much potential!" I ate it up. I felt important, because of this *maybe* that people saw in me. I was banking on a big maybe, and I was always striving for that maybe. The problem with potential, though, is you never know when you've "made it." You may have more in the tank, more to achieve. More attagirls and pats on the back to strive for.

The possibility of unmet potential leaves us terrorized. We don't want to leave anything on the table, but the problem is that we never know how much potential we (or something) have. Potential is by nature immeasurable. And when we can't measure something, we can never know if we've arrived.

There is a certain "never-endingness" to everything we do. The internet never ends. It's on a permanent scroll for a reason. The people who design the technological environments we use every day are incentivized to keep us there. If we don't have the option of ever reaching the bottom, maybe at least some of us will never stop scrolling.

Parenthood never ends, or at least the heart work of it doesn't. When you have a child, you're invested for life. You absolutely care how that little booger turns out. There is always another bottom to wipe, another lunch to make, another spelling test to help with. And that doesn't even speak to the prayers on that child's behalf or the nights you stay awake wondering if you're enough for them.

The work we do has far-off fruit. We don't live in an era where we get a lot of satisfaction from our day at work. We don't produce a widget and then clock out and go home to dinner. If you told a worker from the 1960s how little time we feel we have today, they might think we're crazy, since we live in a time of expedited everything. Amazon Prime shipping revolutionized the idea of spending and shopping and waiting. We binge on television shows, preferring not to have to wait for the next episode. On social media, we can keep up (however marginally) with thousands of friends at one time.

According to a December 2014 article in *The Economist*, there is a "distinct correlation between privilege and pressure."[1] We may earn more money, but we can never earn more time. And because we're working jobs that are less physically taxing, we actually enjoy and find more fulfillment in our work today. This leads us to finding our identity in our work and allowing it to bleed out inordinately into other parts of our life. Time, then—our least renewable resource—feels all the more valuable (and elusive).

What we are really feeling is pressure. We aren't actually busier. We want to maximize everything, milk it for efficiencies. Opportunity cost rises the more you have access to. To choose nothing feels ungrateful and unwise.

Our privilege causes us to have anxiety over the seemingly endless ways we can mess up.

Jennie Allen, the visionary leader of IF:Gathering, says the question she hears most from women is, "I want to please God—I just don't know what he wants from me?"[2] That's the question of "potential." We have the potential to please God, but what does that require and how will we know when we've arrived?

Almost all Americans today have a higher standard of living than the vast majority of every human who ever walked the planet. But it's not enough. We're still striving for more. To do more, to be more. Author Gregg Easterbrook writes, "Our lives are characterized by too much of a good thing—too much to eat, to buy, to watch and to do, excess at every turn."[3] But what if there were more?

INFORMATION CAN DISTRACT
US FROM *KNOWLEDGE*

The information we have access to has exploded in my lifetime. When I was a kid, I would plod into the school library and make my way to an oaken card catalog that I had to stand on my tip-toes to access. I loved every single thing about the library. I loved Mrs. Smith, the quintessential small-town librarian whose white hair was permed into short, tight curls and who was wearing holiday-themed jewelry. She was like a real-life Ms. Frizzle.

I loved the paint bucket full of paint stirrers with Fishers Elementary penned down the side in Sharpie. We used those to hold space when we removed a book from the shelf. We learned the Dewey Decimal System, and the best books had index cards so worn that they were as soft as cloth. We leafed through matching sets of encyclopedias, updated at least every other year. The boundary of information at our fingertips was finite, found within the walls of the wonderful library. I still experience awe when I stand in a library, so wildly full of words and ideas. But back then, there was comfort too. There was a safe end to the information I could access.

These scenes seem antiquated now, left over from a long-ago time tinged with a dusty, vintage filter. To say that our access to information has exploded doesn't really capture the cataclysmic change. On April 23, 2005, the very first video was uploaded to YouTube. Now "more video is uploaded to YouTube in one month than the 3 major US networks created in 60 years."[4] An iPhone has more computing power than all of NASA had in the 1960s.[5] And to underline, bold, and italicize the point of just how much information is out there, you can download the entirety of the actual code of the Apollo Guidance Computer for free on GitHub.[6]

According to Martin Doyle, CEO and founder of DQ Global, a data quality software company, "In essence, data is raw. It has not been shaped, processed or interpreted. It is a series of 1s and zeros that humans would not be able to read (and nor would they want to). It is disorganized and unfriendly. Once data has been processed and turned into information, it becomes palatable to human readers. It takes on context and structure. It becomes useful for businesses to make decisions, and it forms the basis of progress."[7]

Scientists even developed a hierarchy for processing data called the DIKW (data, information, knowledge, wisdom) pyramid.[8] At the bottom, the most unformed and unsorted, is *data*. Next is *information*, which is data that has been processed. *Knowledge* is data that has been processed into information and then organized into some sort of structure. And finally, *wisdom* (which is what God says we should pursue) is at the very top of the DIKW pyramid.

Taking in all of this data can be exhausting. It keeps us from other pursuits. The thing is, because our brains are essentially computers (more accurately, computers attempt to mimic our brains), it cannot help but process the data we encounter. And we encounter a lot of data. IBM estimates that "90 percent of the data in the world today has been created in the last two years alone."[9] We are at an unprecedented time in history, because though the temptation for distraction has always been there, the volume, velocity, and variety of information haven't.

In his book *Christianity for Modern Pagans*, Peter Kreeft writes these insightful words in response to a question he posed: "Why doesn't anybody have any time today? Where did all the time go?"[10]

We *want* to complexify our lives. We don't *have* to, we *want* to. We want to be harried and hassled and busy. Unconsciously, we want the very thing we complain about. For if we had leisure, we would look at ourselves and listen to our hearts and see the great gaping hole in our hearts and be terrified, because that hole is so big that nothing but God can fill it.

So we run away like conscientious little bugs, scared rabbits, dancing attendance on our machines, our slaves, our masters. We think we want peace and silence and freedom and leisure, but deep down we know that this would be unendurable to us."[11]

Our minds just get overwhelmed with all the data and information available to us. And it truly does distract and numb us. Our minds will eventually just give up and glaze over.

Babies are famous for this. Their brains are immature. Everything is new to them, and they soak up the world eagerly, like a sponge. However, their brains also are extremely sensitive to being overwhelmed. With Cooper, my second son, this paradox came as a surprise to me, and it took me a while to figure out what the problem was.

Cooper was, and still is, the most voracious observer. He'd perk right up when he heard voices. His eyes would lock on to anything bright and moving, and he always resisted rest when we were out. When Cooper was about six months old, I realized it was getting harder to tote him around like I had when he was a newborn. Noah, my firstborn, was about two and a half at this point, and we tried to get out of the house a lot to stay busy. But Cooper, because he took in the world around him with such vigor, would also peter out quickly.

He'd first let out a warning sign—a cry that sounded like he'd been pinched. And then he'd just remain irritable and difficult to settle. Finally, he'd nosedive into my shoulder and nuzzle in. With so much hunger for the world, he would become overstimulated, and after that cry of immediate distress and then irritability, he would become a little baby zombie. The world had completely overwhelmed him.

One of the most effective ways to get a lie to slip through undetected is to wrap it up with a lot of other unnecessary and complicated information. If you can overwhelm someone, they are less defensive about what information they're taking in. There's no point in trying to control the narrative; now the modus operandi is to just flood the environment with more than what one's mind can process. "Information glut is the new censorship," says Zeynep Tufekci of the University of North Carolina, who is an expert on the social implications of emerging technologies, especially when it comes to political and cultural dynamics.[12]

COMPARISON DISTORTS

A couple of years ago, I was asked to speak at a local outlet of a national conference. I gave a short talk on the civic engagement of millennial women and then joined a small group of attendees at one of the tables that peppered the room. Everyone had been asked to discuss the topic just presented, and seeing that I was the presenter, it was more than a little awkward.

After a few seconds of silence as we shifted in our chairs, a middle-aged man in a Carhartt jacket spoke up. He said—and I can still hear it clear as day—"I just hate how women feel like they need to measure up to Rihanna on Instagram."

This comment was so out of place that it felt like a scratched record, and we all whipped our heads around to face him. I stifled a giggle, because, really, did he just say we all want to be like Rihanna?

A woman named Joy (I looked at her name tag) cleared her throat. She had the look of a tired woman who was trying to do a good job at just about everything. What she said stunned me into nine months of introspection: "Honestly, I don't think we hold Rihanna up as our idol. I think we try to measure up to other Christian women we see on social media—those women who are doing 'big things' for Jesus. It looks important, and who doesn't want to serve the Lord?"

She had just been to a national leadership event and said she talked to many women who had similar concerns. You could tell it was weighing heavily on her spirit.

On our phones, we have a portal into the lives of any one of 2.62 billion people in the world who use social media.[13] We can see our favorite movie star, not relegated just to the covers of magazines anymore, but creating her own content and publishing multiple times a day. We can peek into the day of our neighbors down the street, getting a glimpse at rooms of their houses we may never see in real life. We can follow the people we love, and we can follow the people we love to hate.

But the most tempting, I believe, is to look at women who are quite like us. We see them buying clothes that look like ours but are a little more expensive and cooking food that's like ours but maybe tastes better. We see her serving, leading, and growing, and we may be tempted to feel that our lives don't measure up anymore.

The university I attended regularly lauds "world changers"— Christians who have done big things for the Lord. There is even a little memorial in the library with the busts of these distinguished few. The problem with everyone thinking they need to change the world, though, is that very few of us ever really do that in a global kind of way.

The worlds we change are the tiny microworlds at our table, over the backyard fence, in the waiting room at the hospital ER. That kind of world changing isn't as glamorous as a speaking tour or a nonprofit start-up or a side hustle. But that kind of world-changing work is how Jesus operated. He never sought a platform and actually often absolutely rejected the attention (see such passages as Matthew 9:30; Mark 1:43–44; 3:12; 5:43; 8:30; and others).

Our reality is distorted by comparison. We're discouraged by what we would be *thrilled* about if we didn't have anything else to compare it to. How sad is that? What we would consider an absolute success and a blessing to us and others in any other situation suddenly feels pale and small when we see the bright lights, hair, and makeup of someone else's service.

BUSYNESS EXHAUSTS

I live in the suburbs, where the temptation is to constantly add more and more to our lives. We are allured by an upward trajectory. More work, more money, more house, more cars, more kids, more kids' sports, more everything. This kind of living can make us frantic, even when we're actively aware of it and fighting against the norm. I am a frantic woman when I'm not careful. Just by virtue of the very nature of my life with four boys means I've got a lot on my plate. But when we elevate our activities, errands, and commitments to too high a place, we're in danger of losing our peace.

We were never meant for the kind of harried living our culture has deemed normal. I don't know the way to change the pace of our society, but I do know how to personally resist it. I am not a guru or a wellness coach. I just know that God desires that "normal" life includes periods of rest, reflection, and opportunities for awe and restoration. He knew we'd need this, because left on our own, we can spin ourselves into quite a pickle. He knew the care of our soul would demand downtime every seventh day. He knew that if we got our engines going and didn't stop, we'd completely forget who we are, whose we are, why we're here, and where we're going.

Think about that for a moment. It's a biblical edict that one-seventh of our lives should be spent resting—and not even sleeping! Just resting. Just taking in the work that God has done on our behalf. When we rest—when we embrace Sabbath-rest—we are accepting that God is working on our behalf on something we can't sustain on our own. We are agreeing with Him that His provision is abundantly enough for us, that we can't imagine we could do it any better.

Even our Christmas cards can reveal a dangerous dependency on ourselves. The very greetings we send out to celebrate the birth of Jesus, who came to do what we couldn't manage, is glorifying our busyness instead of Him. There has been a tremendous increase during the past fifty years in those Christmas letters of phrases like "we're busy," "we've had a busy year," and "we've just got such crazy schedules."[14]

But this is what happens when we're so busy. We run ourselves ragged and leave little in the tank for spiritual matters. We act like we believe we have to do it on our own. We act like we believe it's *better* if we do it on our own. Listening to Christian radio while driving through Chick-fil-A on the way to small group isn't enough for spiritual formation. You can't just do "Christian" things; you have to submit and surrender your soul to God.

Author Tim Kreider writes, "Busyness serves as a kind of existential reassurance, a hedge against emptiness."[15] Isn't that the truth? When I'm busy, I feel indispensable. I feel almost godlike in my importance. But you must lay down your life and everything in it, or you're going to burn out. You're going to hit the point of exhaustion, and that's not what God wants from you.

JESUS IS OUR SANCTUARY

We go to church in a warehouse kind of building where the auditorium is painted black and we have a monthly rotating set design. I absolutely adore our church body, and our building is our home. It's great; it's fine. The building is nothing fancy and very utilitarian. I'm grateful that our church leadership stewards our money for priorities that go beyond a fancy building for our congregation. It suits our needs and the needs of the many small children we have space for.

But have you ever been in an old church building that just *felt* holy? Ancient churches were built for a totally different purpose. They weren't built for nursery rooms and offices for the pastors as much as they were built as a reflection of our Creator God. The church building itself, not just the work within it, was set apart. Every flying buttress and marble arch were to the glory of God.

Have you ever tiptoed in the silence of an empty, cavernous cathedral? The quiet and stillness are cocooning. It's cool inside. It's dimly lit and calming, and its spaciousness is inviting. I've found this to be true about Jesus too.

It's Jesus Himself, not just the work we do for Him, that is set apart. He is our very sanctuary (see Isaiah 8:14: "He will be a holy place"). Jesus doesn't just give us peace; He is our peace (Ephesians 2:14). When we find our home in Him, we will find the soul-deep quiet that will change our hearts and our lives. He wants to give us rest from our noise, from our busyness, from our numbness. This is His invitation: "Come to me, all you who are weary and burdened, and I will give you rest. Take my yoke upon you and learn from me, for I am gentle and humble in heart, and you will find rest for your souls" (Matthew 11:28–29).

The great news is that even though the world is not going to start spinning more slowly any time soon, all it takes is anchoring yourself in Christ. He is the One who is, was, and always will be. You get to become more like Him as you grow, and quiet, calm minds are a fruit of abiding in Him. You're not left spinning on your own. You have a Holy Helper who is outside of time and space to slow your spinning and to walk with you in all your days to come.

CHAPTER FIVE

We Try to Go It Alone

God made us: invented us as a man invents an engine. A car is made to run on gasoline, and it would not run properly on anything else. Now God designed the human machine to run on Himself. He Himself is the fuel our spirits were designed to burn, or the food our spirits were designed to feed on . . . God cannot give us a happiness and peace apart from Himself, because it is not there. There is no such thing.

C. S. LEWIS, *MERE CHRISTIANITY*

One day, my friend Page told me something that made me practically fall off my chair. I was shocked. I was moved. And I've been thinking about it for the last two years.

We were sitting cross-legged at Bible study, and she wondered out loud whether in training our children to be independent, we were leading them to be less like Christ. She was musing aloud about the implications of raising children who believe they can do it all on their own—or worse, that they *should* do it all on their own.

I am one of those people. I can be very proud of my ability to keep it all together. If I'm not careful, I can find value in my independence. I feel more valuable because I'm enough on my own. I don't really need anyone. Apart from the Lord, left to my own devices, I can begin to think this is a *good* character trait—one I should celebrate.

My friend's words snapped me back to reality.

I believe that as a culture we are putting independence and self-sufficiency on an undue pedestal. We prop up these characteristics when instead we should be cheering for those who are willing to make themselves low and vulnerable. We Christians talk all the time about people being *made for community*, but we seem to be most satisfied with ourselves when we don't functionally need one.

If my flesh—my basest desires—had its way, I would move through my day not having any lack, not needing any help, and not getting particularly close to anyone. There's a lot less chance to get hurt when we never put ourselves in someone's debt.

Have you ever had a friend who would never let you do anything for them? They would never ask for help or for $5 to grab a cup of coffee or for a moment of your time. They think they're being easygoing and laid-back. To need nothing—this is how my gut tells me to approach friendships. But the friendship feels a little out of balance, and it's like I'm afraid to stoop low and show that I need help. I think sometimes I do it out of past hurt and an often unrecognized desire to be seen as above others (ouch!).

When I allow myself to indulge the temptation of independence and fakery, the friendships never last long, or at least we don't dig as deep as we could. We are leaving intimacy with each other on the table when we aren't willing to admit need.

Dependence isn't a dirty word. It's a gift. It's a joy. When someone depends on us, we get to use the traits that mirror God the Father in helping, creating, healing, and providing. When we are dependent on someone else, we get to reflect Jesus in His humility, His need, and His willingness.

Not only do we not have intimacy with the Lord by accident or from a neutral stance; *we refuse intimacy with Him.* We have been presented with the option—with the imperative—and we've chosen not to abide in Him.

In all instances of dependence, I've seen a stubborn refusal to allow God to be our strength, our provision, our sustenance. God is actually always there already sustaining us, already providing us with His power, already caring for our daily needs. But we, in our elevated view of ourselves, believe that it's our power and our strength and our know-how that's keeping us going. This is pride, arrogance, and stubbornness that are not lovely.

So if God is always there and always providing these things, if we refuse to acknowledge this and lean into our Provider, then we're refusing intimacy. It is continually offered, and we reject it.

This may seem like a small deal to our American pragmatism. We've been raised to believe that you take care of yourself, that being a burden is the worst, and that only unwise people struggle. However, this is not the case in God's kingdom.

If you're a parent, imagine that your child walks around claiming that everything they had they had earned. Imagine that they acted like it was their hard work that put a roof over their heads. Imagine that they strutted around and only made time for you when it was scheduled. Every morning they ate breakfast with you, but it was rushed and routine, and it was carried out in a spirit of ungratefulness.

And as life-changing as it is when we apply this idea to *human* relationships, I believe it is key to our relationship with *God*. As long as we think we're managing just fine without God, we'll never fully submit to Him. Dependence means we are unable to make it on our own without someone or something else.

But are you functionally able to do without God? Have you set up your life safely within the parameters of your own ability? Do your days run on the inside of the borders of your physical energy? Your emotional bandwidth? Your intellectual ability? Do you operate in a way that is wise in the world's eyes about finances or career or security? Do you have it all together?

What I've found is that when I fully rely on God, I'm also subjecting myself to rely on people. And our culture has given us the message that this is bad. So in my life, to get to the end of myself, I had to do some reverse engineering and rewiring of my life and my brain.

This past spring, I was walking on the campus of Calvin College wearing dirty jeans, last night's pajama T-shirt, and my favorite denim jacket that matched my jeans just a little too closely. I was wearing this strange mix of clothes because I was woefully unprepared for the early spring weather in Michigan.

I was in Grand Rapids on Calvin's campus for the biannual Festival of Faith and Writing. But I had sat on the fence of indecision so long that by the time I decided for sure to go, all the nearby hotels had filled up.

My independent nature—the part of my flesh that doesn't want to rely on God or anyone else—didn't want to put other people out, and I was prepared to stay in an outlying area and drive in each day for the conference. I was also prepared to pay more. My ever-practical husband did not think this was a cute idea. He couldn't fathom why I'd stay alone, pay more money, and drive further just to avoid having to ask for help.

Mike and I have been doing a dance lately—better to say, I've been trying clumsily to follow his lead. He's been gently trying to convince me to get open, get needy, get into the deep bits of life with some girls. I'm great at living my life as a pretty open book, but I'm not great about being known in my weakness. Being weak and in need of help is not where I like to dwell, as not lovely as that is to admit.

So Mike and I struck a deal. He said if I asked five friends if they had a floor I could crash on, then he'd let me off the hook and book a too-expensive, too-far-away, less-fuss hotel for me. After all, the only one I'd be putting out was me. I absolutely did not want to toy with this exercise. But I knew the deep resistance I felt was a good indicator that I needed to need, even if I didn't want to. Yet the thing we dare not do is often the thing we *must* do to obey God.

I asked two friends, who connected me with two others—and *boom*, I had a COUCH, no less. God is a "more" kind of giver. I opened myself up; I asked; and I received. *I don't like to ask things of people, and I'm wondering if that's tied to not asking things of God too.* Is my intimacy with God stunted because I am only reluctantly intimate with people?

The life I want is not at the end of eighty years of self-sufficiency. It's lived in the day-to-day experiences of being needed and needing others. It's in the soul tie we get tangled up in when we share our lives, our desires, and our cares with others. It's difficult to be pulled and stretched when we're woven up into each other's days, but it's good and necessary for the Christian life and for the transmission of the good news.

I have to teach myself that it's okay to need people. I have to remind myself that I don't *always* need margin—or even excess. I have to remind myself that Jesus Himself told me that I didn't need to—and shouldn't—store things up in an imaginary silo (Luke 12:16–21; see also Matthew 6:19–21).

I have a friend who is terrified to run out of physical rest. She is afraid to run on empty. I wonder if she is afraid to find out that God isn't really enough for her, that He won't really come through. I have another friend who is reluctant to marry a good man who is ministry minded. She loves him, but she wonders if she needs a "better provider" as a husband. She's afraid she won't be able to live a life with financial peace and margin. I wonder if she believes that God really provides for her.

What are the boundaries you hold dear? And why do you maintain them?

Perhaps you're thinking, *What if I'm not admired or well-thought-of? What if I can't take care of myself? What if people misunderstand me? What if I can't retire? What if we can't take care of our kids? What if I burn out?*

Here's the good news for you today. We're all very fortunate. We have a God who fights for us (Exodus 14:14), a God who lays out our boundary lines (Psalm 16:6; Acts 17:26), and a God who challenges us to do more with less (Proverbs 15:16; 1 Timothy 6:17–19). We have a God who loves us and cares for us and desires to be needed. We are only fooling ourselves if we think we're doing this all on our own anyway.

The Bible tells us that "the way of fools seems right to them" (Proverbs 12:15). In reality, this is what you are choosing to do when you hold tightly to your independence instead of relying on the Lord.

The other day, my six-year-old son asked me if one of our loved ones was "going their own way." I didn't know what Asher meant at first, so I asked him to explain. "Well," he said, "is she going her own way? Like, she's not going God's way?"

That's all following Jesus means to our little Asher. He knows that to go your own way means to choose self and sin, but to go God's way means you must ask God for help. This is the lowly humility that Jesus modeled for us in His lifetime. What a joy to dependently follow His way instead of our own!

We weren't made to go it alone. We are finite, and every day we have a set number of hours and only a finite reservoir of energy. We cannot manage life if we're not connected to the very vine of our existence. When we decide to go it alone and refuse dependence on God, we will exhaust ourselves. When we exhaust ourselves, we at least want to be pleased and others to be pleased with what we've accomplished.

When we aren't dependent on God, we're charting our own

course. And when we chart our own course, we have the responsibility of being right. No one is leading us except ourselves, and therefore we better be right. When we aren't dependent on the Lord, there can be an incredible loss of peace due to constant second-guessing.

I've lived through a season like this with a young woman I'm close to. Peace nearly evaporated in her life, but she interpreted this lack of peace as God telling her to be more sure, steady, and pragmatic during a season of change. From my perspective, her lack of peace was because she was relying on herself instead of the Lord. She couldn't fathom that God would be leading her somewhere outside of her lived experience.

Why is this peace disappearing? It's not because we aren't called to follow the Lord, for we surely are. This peace is disappearing because we can't stop wondering if we're making the right call.

In college, I hadn't yet grasped the idea of living dependently on God. I let Him be the Lord of my life, but I hadn't yet realized that I needed His sustenance as well. I was living what my friend Emily Freeman calls a "try-hard life."[1] I was outwardly very good and kept all the rules. My ability to keep the rules became a point of pride, and I wanted other people to notice how good I was too.

Other people I know live ostentatious lifestyles because they want people to see what they've acquired through their own hard work. Still others stake their claim on living pragmatic, responsible lives. They want to be acknowledged as being wise in their steadiness.

I long to always be aware of how I am "going my own way." It's a discipline that takes constant growth and course correction. When I wander off the path of righteousness, the path of dependency, I want to tune my heart to become so aware of my lack that I get right back to God's way of radical and intimate reliance. Self-reliance will not lead us to everlasting life, but finding the answer to our own lack in God will discipline our hearts to always be listening for Him.

There is loads of hope to be found here. When we choose the path of reliance on God, we open ourselves up to a God who has filled books with His goodness and His faithfulness. It's good and hopeful to be aware of our lack and our need. When we lean heavily on God, doing nothing out of step with Him, we will be open to the immense ways He can change our minds.

CHAPTER SIX

We're Numb and Sleepwalking

A slothful man . . . is a man who goes through the motions, who flies on automatic pilot. Like a man with a bad head cold, he has mostly lost his sense of taste and smell . . . Other people come and go, but through glazed eyes he hardly notices them. He is letting things run their course. He is getting through his life.

FREDERICK BUECHNER,
WISHFUL THINKING

The days had begun to run together. I woke up, got the kids off to school, managed my day, and came home to repeat the morning routine only in reverse—with the children ending up in bed rather than beginning there. Day after day, the dishes piled up, and then I washed them. The laundry piled up, and then I washed it.

Every day was mostly like the other, and we'd been grateful to not have anything too difficult happen, but that's almost the problem. The days were monotonous, and I'd gotten fairly adept at handling everything. There was nothing too high and nothing too low, but all of the sameness was exhausting. I had begun to feel like my mind was fighting against my spirit, and everything felt like I was trudging through sludge.

Think of a plant. It isn't sentient. It doesn't think; it just reacts to its circumstances. If it's sunny out, it will stretch to its source of life. If it's dry out, it will get wilty and discolored. When it's watered, it pushes back to life as though all it ever needed were water and sunlight. It's alive, but it's not aware.

Or it's like when you reach a point where you realize you haven't been talking about anything other than what you're doing every day. Not how it's going or why you're doing it. Just what is happening. You have no questions to ask anyone else, because you're not even thinking on that level about your own life. You're not being intentional; you're just being.

Because I had let my life and mind get a little busier than I like, I wasn't keeping my aim in the right direction. I was constantly doubting my calling and the methods I was using, and I was feeling like I didn't fit in anywhere. As soon as I got my mind set in one direction, my spirit felt like it folded, and I changed my mind again. Everything felt dull and frantic at the same time. My senses had dulled because I wasn't paying attention, but my mind was running wild with neglect.

Because I know better than to do life alone, I called for help from my friend Susie. I asked if she'd give me a few hours each day over the course of a weekend. I wanted to just be with her, because her joy is contagious. But I was also looking forward to her counsel. So I used some frequent flyer miles and found a flight to Austin, Texas, for a pittance.

The hilarious thing to note here is that I must have been desperate. I don't like putting people out. I don't like asking for help. But somehow I invited myself into her life for the weekend. I'm just now remembering that prior to this weekend, I'd never actually spent time in the flesh with Susie. When she picked me up at the airport, it was the first time she became huggable, 3D flesh in my life. Prior to that, we'd logged hours together over FaceTime and the phone, but we'd never really squeezed each other.

I wandered around Austin and met with Susie here and there. I devoured snacks she had delivered to my hotel room, and I thought hard about some questions she'd prepared for my time at the hotel. Susie is always watching for God and watching out for other people. I desire to live with my eyes wide open, like Susie does.

We spent time just driving around Austin, which is hazardous, if you ask Susie. She's lived in Austin all her life and watched it go from being a quiet college town to the stylish, techy hub it is today. While we drove around and popped into different shops, Susie asked me what I had done for fun when I was a little girl. She wanted to know what brought me joy, what made me come alive, what stopped time when I was a tiny little Hayley.

My immediate answer was that I loved going to the art supply store. While the Austin vista blurred by my car window, I could picture myself back there, sitting cross-legged on the gray industrial carpet, pulling every shade of green paint off the racks. I remember bursting at the possibility of what I could create with these few small supplies.

After a few delicious shared meals, a stop at an art supply store—she swore up and down she needed to go there anyway—and some time at her house, our time together was drawing to a close. It was my last night in Austin, and while I was starting to come alive again, I hadn't had any big breakthroughs.

I wasn't disappointed, but I was expectant as we climbed into a high booth at a place that served burgers and fancy sodas. Susie is the kind of woman who asks great questions, and I was hoping she'd saved some doozies for our last supper.

"What are ten things God is doing in your life right now to woo you?" Susie asked as a softball sort of question. This was not supposed to be one of the doozies.

I searched my brain, and it felt empty. As I recognized the humming numbness of my mind, tears welled up in my eyes. I had no idea.

I had no idea what God was doing to woo me. I knew that God loved me, because that's what I remembered from all my years of reading Scripture. I mostly believed that God loved me, and it's a good thing, since I spent my days telling other people to believe it.

But it was clear I was missing it. I was missing how God was moving in my life—in the right here and the right now. If my job is to enjoy God and give Him glory, then I was snoozing on the job. I had to admit to Susie that I couldn't name *one* way that God was wooing me, loving me actively—let alone ten. I was living the consequences of being spiritually unaware of God's love and movement in my life and in the world around me.

Without knowing it, because it's just who she is, Susie had asked me the one question that got to the marrow of the matter. Her question that was supposed to be a light and fluffy one—well, God ended up using that question like a laser to expose this spiritual sleep in my life.

That night at the burger joint was my wake-up call. Amid the din of the other diners, it was like Jesus whispered, "It's time to wake up, babe"—like a mother does to her child in the morning before school. I could practically feel Him reach in, brush the sleep out of my eyes, and gently shake me awake. This wake-up call was Him wooing me, and I was not going to miss it.

When we go to sleep, it isn't all bad; we just lose our intentionality. We lose our ability to see outside of ourselves and can't bring into focus the blur of what God is doing in the world.

This would not be the first time Jesus tenderly roused a girl out of a deep sleep. In Mark 5:38–42, we peer into a moment in Jesus' ministry where He is asked to come and heal a girl who is presumed to be dead. She's the preteen daughter of a synagogue leader named Jairus.

When they came to the home of the synagogue leader, Jesus saw a commotion, with people crying and wailing loudly. He went in and said to them, "Why all this commotion and wailing? The child is not dead but asleep." But they laughed at him.

After he put them all out, he took the child's father and mother and the disciples who were with him, and went in where the child was. He took her by the hand and said to her, *"Talitha koum!"* (which means "Little girl, I say to you, get up!"). Immediately the girl stood up and began to walk around (she was twelve years old). At this they were completely astonished.

Consider this your wake-up call. If you've been moving through a season of life where nothing is too high and nothing is too low, maybe you've been lulled into a spiritual sleep. Let me ask you to think about how God has been wooing you lately. Make a list of ten ways.

Susie sees God's care and affection in the trees and the birds. Maybe you see God wooing you in the way you've read five articles this week—and they all pricked your heart and are pointing in one solid direction. Maybe you received good news just in the nick of time. Perhaps God woos you in the quiet of the night.

How is He showing His love for you today in real time? How is He moving in your life? Do you even see? Are you following Him?

Talitha koum! Little girl, get up!

HOW CAN WE WAKE UP TO WHAT THE LORD IS UP TO?

Take back wonder. When was the last time God impressed you? I promise you, it's not that God is becoming less impressive, but that we are not easily impressed. We need to practice awe and wonder, but that means getting outside of ourselves and our day-to-day surroundings. We need to establish what Walter Brueggemann has termed a "prophetic imagination."[1] We need to be able to envision a reality that isn't here yet, but has been promised by God. Are you feeling cynical? There isn't a YouTube video out there that shocks us anymore. We need to keep our eyes open to the wonder and promises of God. He promises to change our lives in the here and now, as well as in the hereafter.

Shift your lens of focus to others. Our cynicism can lead to a profound self-focus. We can start to believe we have to watch out for ourselves. When that happens, I start thinking of myself and my place in God's kingdom more than my God Himself. What starts with the best of intentions can lead to ruminating on my thoughts, my needs, and my desires. Our enemy sometimes uses our best intentions for our downfall. Move the microscope off your own life, off your own thoughts and feelings, and onto the needs of others.

Center yourself on your purpose. When we don't have our eyes open to what God is doing in the world, we can become discouraged and self-focused. And before we know it, we've lost the vision for what the whole point was to begin with. We start to wake up in the morning wondering what the point of it all is anyway. We may try to inject extra meaning by adding more things to our schedule or making ourselves more indispensable to others. Nothing will fill this void though. When we lose our sense of purpose, it's a profound loss. It's not a permanent loss, but it is one that will need to be rightly redeemed and reordered by God.

Unplug. The other week, I felt like I was slipping back into a dark lack of wonder. Maybe it was winter's approach that had me in a funk. I wasn't paying attention to what God was doing, and I was becoming more self-focused and discouraged. I texted Susie, because she's the most wonder-aware person I know. She's always seeing little love notes from God, and I wish I had the spiritual eyes she has.

Her first encouragement was to turn off anything that required power to connect me to other people. I needed to be connecting with other people face-to-face or in the pages of a book. My computer, my television, and my phone needed a rest as much as I did.

Then she told me to go outside. She reminded me that seeing the bigness of God helps me see what a blessedly small part of it I am. It's always wonderful to get a right view of ourselves in the world. The cool breeze and the twigs snapping under my feet keep me grounded in place and time.

It's no big surprise that when our attention is focused on a four-inch screen, we can get a myopic view of life and lose sight of what God is doing in our lives. But this is a simple reset, and it's shocking how quickly the act of unplugging and getting outside can change our view. We're able to see the bigger world—how much bigger it really is. Our big, round globe of an earth looks flat to our eyes—that's how small we really are. And God exists outside time and space in a place of glory all by Himself.

All we need to do is lift up our eyes.

Look for God. God is ever with us. He's never, ever gone anywhere. We just need to look around and see what He's up to.

To wake up to what the Lord is up to, we need to go back and remember the things that have happened in the past. When we want to see what God is doing in our lives and in the world, we must look to what He did in the past. In our lives, in the culture, in the world. How do we develop kingdom eyes? We must adopt an eternal perspective.

Look to the margins. Jesus didn't seek earthly power while He was here in the flesh. He went to the margins, where the lowly, displaced, unwanted, and disgraced were. This is countercultural for us who are indoctrinated with the ideas of "leadership," "power," and "world changing." However, the kind of world-changing work Jesus did was always with the least of these (Matthew 25:31–46). He wasn't sitting in meetings with Herod, enjoying the perks of having the ear of a king. He wasn't out collecting votes to pass new laws.

Jesus was busy healing a woman who had been bleeding for twelve years, making her ceremonially unclean for society (Matthew 9:20–22). Jesus was spending His time allowing a sinful woman to soak His feet with wildly expensive perfume and then dry them with her hair (Luke 7:36–39). Jesus met the weakest, most outcast members of society and then instructed them to tell no one that He healed them (see Mark 1:43–44, for example).

Jesus was busy in a no-man's-land on the outskirts of town among the riffraff. He's still busy with these same kinds of people.

My friend Jace is a documentary filmmaker in Nashville, Tennessee. I recently watched some footage of a new film he's working on. In Nashville, as in many temperate cities, the homeless population is booming. Jace met with, got to know, and filmed scores of men in a hidden forested encampment downtown at St. Cloud Hill, a self-governed tent community.

The men in this encampment exhibited deep faith that God would provide, all while living with next to nothing. Who knows the reasons for their plight—and do we even know why most of the people who needed Jesus were in theirs?

Jesus has moved on behalf of the people at the margins throughout history, and He most definitely is still moving now.

Our eyes can be immediately opened and focused on this spiritual reality if we only get to the outskirts of town, where the down-and-out gather.

SIGNS FROM PSALM 119 THAT YOU'RE COMING ALIVE

Being awake and aware, opening your kingdom eyes—these things will change you. When you answer the call of "Little girl, get up!" you will come alive. The best example in Scripture is King David. He was honest and could feel everything. He told God about it all, and he was hungry to know what God was doing in the world.

Psalm 119 has great spiritual significance, but these verses from Eugene Peterson's paraphrase (MSG) stand out in particular:

> I'm single-minded in pursuit of you;
> > don't let me miss the road signs you've posted.
> > (verse 10)

When you are awake to what God is doing, you don't want to miss a single thing. Your eyes are open, scanning the horizon, like they would be if you were driving in an unfamiliar place. You don't want to miss your next turn! You will seek God like a bloodhound, trained on only one thing: to know Him and make Him known.

> I delight far more in what you tell me about living
> > than in gathering a pile of riches. (verse 14)

You're eager to hear God's Word. You want the Spirit to be always illuminating more about God. Your time and heart's energy are spent knowing God more than on your career or on managing your possessions. The thrust of your life is to be with the Lord.

> Open my eyes so I can see
>> what you show me of your miracle-wonders.
>>> (verse 18)

You believe that God is still active and moving today. You risk appearing foolish (or feeling foolish) to believe that God is truly invested and involved in your life today. You believe that every good gift comes from Him (James 1:17) and take mental note of all He's doing and has done.

> Help me understand these things inside and out
>> so I can ponder your miracle-wonders. (verse 27)

You're like my sons with their dad, my husband, Mike. They want to know every single thing he's doing and why. They want to know, because they want to know their dad. They also want to know, because they believe they can become more like their dad. Think of going to work with God like He's your dad—and you keep pace right behind Him, asking about every facet of the family business.

> And I'll stride freely through wide open spaces
>> as I look for your truth and your wisdom.
>>> (verse 45)

When you're awake, you're not afraid to go. Spiritual growth always pushes you to the unknown void. You can't yet see what's ahead of you, because there is so much. As Psalm 119:105 tells us, God only illuminates our feet, our next step. But you trust Him, and you'll go in search of more of what He's doing.

> Then I'll tell the world what I find,
>> speak out boldly in public, unembarrassed.
>>> (verse 46)

Once you know Him, once you trust Him, once your eyes are open and you're wide awake, you'll start to plant the seeds of truth wherever you go. You can't help but tell your friends and family of the miracle-wonders God is doing in your life and theirs.

> You are good, and the source of good;
>> train me in your goodness. (verse 68)

You'll see that God is good. Finally, truly, really. You'll have chased after Him when you come to the end of yourself, and that's where you'll find you can really trust in His goodness. He is good; He does good; and He is where all good comes from. You'll want Him to show you how to be more like Him.

> Oh, how I love all you've revealed;
>> I reverently ponder it all the day long. (verse 97)

Once He's shown you, it's all you can think about. It's what you wake up hoping to see more of, and it's the thanksgiving that's on your lips when your head hits the pillow. This is what it's like to be spiritually alive and aware.

I was thinking today about how I live for little, exciting cultural events. As I write this, the world is all eyes on Britain's royal family. Harry and Meghan are getting married, and Kate and Will just had a baby boy. And today I'm refreshing People.com every five minutes to find out the new little prince's name. I look for these fresh bits of fun news to feel alive and connected with other people. But living awake and paying attention to the Lord provide the best kind of excitement in the world. The Lord delivers every day in His affection and care for us, but it is up to us to pay attention to the delight.

CHAPTER SEVEN

Our Wounds keep Us Sidelined

There are many ways to perish, or to flourish.

How old pain, for example, can stall us at the threshold
of function.

Memory: a golden bowl, or a basement without light.

For which reason the nightmare comes with its painful
story and says: *you need to know this.*
MARY OLIVER, "EVIDENCE"

On my left was my dear friend and mentor Susie. And around our circular booth was my friend Jess and a handful of other close friends. We were sitting in a fancy hotel restaurant, excited about the half-off happy hour appetizers. My heart was heavy after a long weekend of work events, and I was excited to have time with my mentor-friend, for whom I'll always joyfully make time.

Susie is an excellent question asker. It's one of her spiritual gifts, I think. She asks incisive questions that make me think of when Jesus meets Andrew for the first time. John the Baptist is standing with two of his followers, and Jesus walks by. John says, "Look, the Lamb of God!" (John 1:36). John's job was to pave the way for Jesus, and all great mentors would do well to have this mind-set. Set the stage for Jesus; point to Jesus; call people to follow not you but Jesus.

When John the Baptist's disciples started following Jesus, His first question for them was "What do you want?" (John 1:38). The original language gives more color to the word. It means, "What are you *aimed at*? Where is your life *headed*? Jesus wanted to know what they were after in following Him.

These are the kinds of questions that Susie asks: "What do you want? Where is your heart aimed?" I don't specifically remember what Susie asked me that day, but it set in motion an afternoon that blurred into an evening that is etched into my sensual memory.

I can remember what the air smelled like, what my tears tasted like, and how time seemed to slow to a crawl.

This weekend was at a women's ministry gathering, and Jess and I were long overdue for a heart-to-heart. We were at the end of the weekend, so we were tired from travel, wrung-out from meetings, and just getting ready to launch our first book. We were about to release *Wild and Free*, and Susie asked us how we were doing—like, really doing at a heart level.

For some reason, in response to Susie's question, we launched into the answer to that question right across the table, in front of an audience of good friends. We spoke honestly and frankly, because we love each other. This should have been a safe place to process, with wise loved ones literally flanking us. Jesus' kinds of questions tend to touch something deep inside us, pushing us to need to be closer to Him.

In spite of this safe spot, something visceral snuck up on me and turned this from a helpful and edifying conversation into something we'll always call "the unhappy happy hour." I felt backed into a corner and condemned, although I'm *absolutely certain* that was not the intention at all.

I snotted and snorted and used every person's cocktail napkin to wipe my nose between extended crying jags. I am a fairly steady person emotionally, but this was uncontrollable. It welled up out of the deepest part of myself with the intensity of Old Faithful. I couldn't explain it, and my sobbing response far outweighed even the feelings I was experiencing in the moment. It was such an outsized response that it confused me, which led to more crying.

Eventually, I had to go to an event for authors, agents, and editors, so Jess and I hugged it out, affirmed all the things we loved about each other, and Ubered to a drugstore for some redness-relieving eye drops. I still felt emotionally off balance and stunned at the way it had all unfolded. I couldn't figure out why I had reacted so strongly. I'm sure I wasn't the only one surprised by my emotional expression, but no one else seemed stressed about the content of the conversation.

I flew home the next day in a state of shock. I didn't know what had happened and what in the world it all meant. I kicked around the events of that night in my head and heart for months, but I still had no idea why I responded from the core of myself.

Months later, I was talking with Susie over FaceTime about something else entirely when I mentioned that my dad used to drive me to eat at sit-down restaurants when he had something hard to talk about. I'm not sure why he did this. Maybe he thought it was like a spoonful of sugar that would make the "medicine" go down easier. Whatever his reasons, it had the effect of making me feel trapped, exposed, and called out, with all my emotions on display for all around us to see as they were trying to enjoy their all-you-can-eat salad bar. When he took me to a public place to deliver difficult news, it also left me feeling like there was no space for my reaction, and maybe that was by design.

Susie responded, "You mean like 'the unhappy happy hour'?" Once again, I was stunned. Yes. At "the unhappy happy hour," thirty-year-old Hayley felt exactly like twelve-year-old Hayley in her hardest times.

Over time, I've begged the Lord for insight about this night, and He's been good to give it to me. I think my response to my childhood's unhappy dinners out was to try to cover my vulnerabilities and deflect attention any way I could. I felt exposed and lacked any sort of control or autonomy, so I just tried to get the spotlight off me as quickly as possible. And at "the unhappy

happy hour," it dredged back up all those feelings. When Susie asked how Jess and I were doing after a heavy season of working together, our frank conversation felt necessary but difficult. This decades-old wound that whispered that I was exposed and out of control when pressed on in a public place by a loved one reemerged in 2017.

I didn't know this wound was still affecting me almost twenty years later. To be honest, I'd pushed it so far down that it took an outsized emotional response to an innocuous conversation to bring it to the light. I wonder if you have some of those wounds too. I'm guessing you have some that you've thrown a Band-Aid on and forgotten about, completely unaware that they're festering and going untreated.

When we have a wound (spiritual or otherwise), it won't heal unless we tend to it. This seems like common sense, but it is shocking how often we leave the invisible wounds of our spirit alone. They don't heal well, and they cause us problems for decades.

When we leave a wound untended to, unhealed, it is fertile ground for Satan to plant a seed of infection. He plants and buries a lie deep inside our wound.

In my case, I felt like my dad was shining a spotlight on my flaws, and Satan then planted a lie that I wasn't safe when being confronted. I began to believe that every kind of relational "sit-down" would end with me on the receiving end of criticism and condemnation.

So we become wounded by something that probably wasn't even meant to hurt us. It wasn't likely malicious or done on purpose, but we're wounded nonetheless. When we're wounded and don't let God heal that wound, Satan sees it as a nice dark place to plant his deceptive seed. Then we begin to believe that lie.

- **The wound:** My dad took me to a nice restaurant to tell me he and my mom were getting a divorce.
- **The lie:** Every time someone wants to connect with me relationally, it will be painful.
- **The false belief:** Intimate relationships are unsafe.

From our beliefs, we form our thoughts. Our beliefs inform everything that runs through our minds. And we all know that our thoughts dictate our behavior.

If you're walking around with unhealed wounds, it essentially means you're walking around unhealthy. You are susceptible to further infection or injury. You are fresh, fertile ground for the infection of a lie, which can lead to untrue beliefs and bad news loops.

Sometimes wounds are difficult to spot. Wounds of the heart aren't typically like the gunshot wounds we see on medical dramas on television. They don't get immediate attention; they rarely get taken care of right away. Sometimes they're like a pulled muscle—from the outside they're invisible, but on the inside, they're excruciating. Sometimes they're just a little annoying ache that we eventually learn to live with it. We compensate, walk with a limp, or just stop moving in certain ways altogether. We learn to cope so we don't keep reopening the wound but try to live our lives normally even after the damage has been done.

I think we can spot wounds a lot like a doctor would though. Imagine taking a complaint of general ill health to your trusted doctor. You describe to her what's wrong, and it doesn't seem to be anything specific. You have a pain here and some tightness there, and you're just feeling like junk.

She might have you lie down on a table with that awkward,

crinkly paper. She'd have you put your hands over your head in a way that's awfully vulnerable (if you ask me). She might press on your abdomen and ask if it hurts. This is how doctors get to the root of our pain. They can't see inside our bodies, like Ms. Frizzle does in *The Magic School Bus*. Our doctors have to go by what we tell them and how we react to being pressed on, prodded, and poked.

In the same way, we palpate the soft places of our lives and look for any grimaces or tender spots. Oftentimes, our emotions are good indicators of our health.

That night at the Texas dive joint, it was clear that something happened that had hit a sore spot. The cause wasn't immediately obvious to me, and to everyone else it just looked like I'd lost my junk. I couldn't shake what had happened though, and I knew I didn't just lose my junk.

My reaction was so outsized. The tears came so hard and fast that I had to gulp for air. It felt humiliating and acutely, painfully vulnerable. I knew that emotions so strong had to be tied to something deeper. However, it took months of prayer, talking with trusted friends, and ultimately a wise observation from Susie to put two and two together.

If you're looking for ways to identify the wounds you're walking around with, start there. What happened recently that caused you to have an outsized response? What was said that made something gush up from deep inside, an unstoppable force that demands to be seen and heard?

Take note, and ask God to begin to uncover that wound. Ask Him to debride your wound, to clean out any of the infected or dead parts. Ask Him to show up, to hold your hand, and to begin your recovery.

ADDRESSING OUR WOUNDS

So what can we do with our wounds? Jesus gives us a way.

Apply the Salve of Truth Immediately to Our Wounds

When we are wounded, we need to immediately apply the salve of truth. We need to talk back to the lies in our heads with truth. Scripture says that God doesn't make us timid, but gives us power and a sound mind (2 Timothy 1:7). We need to continually take inventory of what is running through our minds and make sure we combat false beliefs with real, lasting truth.

Truth can be quickly found in God's Word, but it's even more effective if it's already part of us. When we memorize Scripture, when we move it deep inside our hearts and down into our bones, it acts like an immune system of sorts. It becomes part of our makeup, our DNA, and the Spirit calls upon it without us even having to think.

The faster we can lay the truth as a covering on our wound, the better. The truth acts like a barrier that Satan's seed just can't penetrate. The Word of God is mightier than any scheme of our enemy. He will not hurt you more than you've already been stung if you put truth over your pain.

Here's a very millennial suggestion: Even if you don't have any particular Scriptures memorized, there is no shame in using Google to find a verse that speaks to your problem. You're not going to be able to just read it, however. This is Scripture that will need to become a part of you for the foreseeable future.

My friend Claire writes the Scripture she's keeping in mind in red lipstick on her mirror. It shocks her every time she looks at it, and she can easily re-create the image in her mind when she needs to recall it.

I keep a box of index cards in my purse to jot down my Scripture "antidotes" in real time. That way, I can review them like a little kid doing math facts flash cards.

I break this down to bite-size mantras for my boys. When we're talking about obedience, sometimes they feel like it's just too hard. So I remind them of 1 John 5:3: "In fact, this is love for God: to keep his commands. And his commands are not burdensome." You could even develop a simpler paraphrase: "To love God, I need to obey God. And what He asks isn't too hard."

Write it everywhere. Underline it in your Bible. Ask your friends to pray it over you.

The truth is not a Band-Aid; it's like a skin graft. It becomes part of you so that you're stronger than you were before the wound.

Change the False Beliefs

False beliefs are the first things that sprout when a lie is planted. You start to buy into the lies that Satan drove deep into your wound. And why wouldn't you? They probably sound true. Satan's lies match the pain from our wound. They confirm with brutality that we're aching. The thing about false beliefs, though, is that the lie may feel right, but it will damage us and not heal us.

Pluck that little bad belief out when it's tiny. You must learn to tell the difference between a flower and a weed. Both look charming when they're small. But like a weed, the roots of a bad belief will grow down deep and spread out wide—and they'll get uglier over time. They'll grow faster and taller than any flower in a garden. They'll choke out any good news in your life. They block out the sun and cause smaller, lovelier growth to wither.

You can change your false beliefs this way too. Notice them when they're small and benign. Take the belief to God and ask

Him if it's bad news or His good news. Ask Him to show you. He will. He's like a master gardener. He wants good things to grow. Once He's shown you that what you're believing doesn't match up with His truth, get as close as you can to the soil, the soft flesh of your wound; pinch it and yank it right out. Don't just break off the ugly top part that everyone can see and leave the root. It'll grow back quickly—more quickly than you ever expected.

Watch for Any New Loops to Begin

Are you noticing any new bad news thoughts popping up? These new things to dwell on can be indicators that something is awry. Anytime there's a shift in the chatter in my brain, I ask why.

Intelligence agencies are constantly collecting information from their agents in the field, their informants, and the computer data being transmitted. They call this information "chatter." They're mining this flow of information to stay abreast of any threats or plans against the nation. They're listening for patterns, repeated phrases, and names of new players. They're often more impressed by a *change* in chatter than they are in any direct thing that was said. They look for shifts in subject matter, in frequency, in volume. The changes tell their own story.

The changes in what we're thinking tell a story too. They can alert us that there has been a wound, or they can tell us we're still hurting from an old hurt. Keep listening to the chatter in your head.

Ask God to help you discern this flow of information like an intelligence agency analyst does. You can become an expert on your own thought life, knowing the good from the bad, the new news from the old news. You can learn the players so you're able to distinguish God's voice from Satan's. Both of them can sound like your own voice, so it's best to learn their tells.

As you analyze the chatter in your mind, here are good questions to ask:

- Does what you're hearing match up with what you know of Scripture? (If not, it's not God.)
- Is this voice condemning? (Not God.)
- Is this voice causing confusion or chaos? (Not God.)
- Is this voice making you timid or paralyzing you? (Not God.)
- Are you asking, "Did God really say?" (Not God.)

If it's God in your head, you can guarantee that what the voice is saying will not go against what He has already revealed in Scripture.

THE HEALING JOURNEY

When I was less than a year old, I was playing underneath my mom's ironing board. She was doing exactly what I now do—talking on the phone while doing the ironing. I did what babies do, and I yanked on the closest thing to me, which was the long cord of the hot iron. The heavy iron, full of water for steaming, fell faster than my mom could grab it, although she certainly tried.

The nose of the iron caught me right on my fat little baby forearm. My mom has always felt horrible about that unforeseeable, unstoppable parenting moment. She cried more than I did that day. Every parent has those moments when harm comes to our kids and we can't stop it from happening.

Thirty years later, I carry a scar from that day. It doesn't hurt, but it's visible. It has stretched out as I've grown, and it has gotten a lot lighter. It has flattened out, but it's still distinctively the shape of the tip of an iron.

I don't have a single memory without this scar, and to me, it's just what my arm looks like. I learned to tell the difference between my right hand and my left because of the two freckles below my left pointer finger and the scar on the forearm of my right arm. The scar became a painless part of me.

We can use our scars to remind us of what God has healed us from. Wounds can't become scars until they're healed. The good news is that once you're only looking at a painless reminder, you've done the hard work of healing. God has seen you through!

Here's what I see as important steps on the healing journey.

Let Your Wound See the Light

I can be a hider. And if I'm not careful, I don't mind if people think better of me than they ought. I prefer to look put together. This reminds me of when we had our first son, Noah. It wasn't long after his birth that my mom and my in-laws came into the room to meet him. As my in-laws walked through the door, I noticed a smear of blood on the handle of the bed—an obvious marker of the run-of-the-mill trauma I'd just endured. But I was mortified, as though that sign of trauma was unmasking the cool-as-a-cucumber vibe I was trying to emit.

Even though I was a first-time mom cuddling my swaddled newborn in one arm, I clamped my other hand over that trace of blood so that no one would see the evidence of the carnage that had occurred. I kept my hand there during the whole visit, even as I passed the baby from one loving family member to another. It seems awfully silly now because of all the life I've lived and all the humility that motherhood has brought me. But at the time, I really thought I could hide the pain by covering the blood.

I try to live honestly. I don't hide my wounds in order to keep other people from being uncomfortable. To hide would be to my detriment. It's not wise, and it will only keep people from being able to care for me and love me like I need it. The truth is, if we don't show the pain, we won't receive the help.

Make Sure Your Wound Heals All the Way

Letting your wound heal halfway is like taking only half of your antibiotics. It's not smart. You risk worse infection or injury down the road. It is worth it to take the time to allow your wound to totally heal.

Athletes are the worst at wanting to get back to the field of play before they're totally healed. They know their bodies and are used to being supremely confident in them. However, you can decimate a healing injury if you stress it too soon. This will push back the recovery and make rehabbing much more difficult.

You don't need a worse recovery or a superbug infecting you later on down the road—one that's tenfold more difficult to heal. Just take the time to heal completely. Let time be on your side.

Don't Put a Band-Aid on the Wound
When You Really Need Surgery

Sometimes we're wounded so badly that we need surgery. We need the severe mercy of the Divine Physician's scalpel to cut away the rot and allow new flesh to grow in its place. Don't give in to the temptation to just slap a Band-Aid on your wound so you can get back to your life. No job, no relationship, no ministry assignment, is more important than your wholeness in the Lord. Let Him restore you, even if the restoration ends up being intense.

Sometimes things won't heal correctly unless some serious work is done. Please take your wellness seriously. Sometimes women have the tendency to shortcut their own healing because it seems frivolous or indulgent. But take this as your permission: *get healthy.* The Lord can and will heal these wounds, and you can start to hear real truth in your mind every day rather than false beliefs running like a news ticker at the bottom of a nightly news show. This is good and worthy work that will yield benefits for the rest of your life and down through generations of other believers.

CHAPTER EIGHT

We Might Not Really Believe

I know many people who profess serious allegiance to Jesus, and claim him as their savior. But, unfortunately, they simply will not take essential scriptures into their soul and body and utilize them . . . The result is that they continue to recycle their failures and make little or no real progress toward the abundance/obedience essential to "walking worthily of the calling wherewith we are called" . . . An essential ingredient is missing, and the order of their mind and life remains other than that of the kingdom.

DALLAS WILLARD,
"THE GOD-FOCUSED MIND"

*N*early five years ago, my husband started to get uncomfortable in his corporate job. He would come home frustrated, unfulfilled, and panicky. It was nonsensical, because he was performing well, even cracking into the top 10 percent of salespeople in his Fortune 500 company. No matter how well he was performing, though, Mike was starting to believe that God was calling him away from his cushy corporate job. We purposed that we were going to follow God's leading as Mike would leave his job, and we would learn about God as our provider. Somehow, for me, having our paycheck automatically deposited every month felt less like God providing than the bank fairy leaving something under our pillow at night.

I'm highly risk-intolerant, but I was confident that God would care for us if Mike left his high-paying role. As fledgling business owners often experience, we had times where money was personally very tight. It felt like we were hovering right on the line between just enough and not enough at all.

Every time our bank account got dangerously low, I felt freaked out and began to scheme how I was going to make a quick buck to cover our shortfall. I was normally able to rustle up enough money that we'd just squeak by, but after doing that month after month, it started to feel wrong in my spirit. For some reason, even though I absolutely don't think it's wrong in all cases, I began to feel that I was being disobedient by not sitting back and letting God show me He could provide.

I intellectually believed that God provided for us, but I was living as though I had to make it happen myself. Month after month, we'd have a little less than what would pay the bills, and when I tried to attack that shortfall through my own hustling, I ended up feeling exhausted, resentful, and defeated. So one day I told Mike that I thought I was being disobedient in my hustling. He agreed, and we decided to see what it would look like to do just what God called us to—this crazy baby business—and see if God really would provide for our needs.

As we got on our knees in our bedroom, the sky was the violet of twilight, and we prayed until the sun had sunk so far that the windows were blacked out. We decided then and there that we would sink or swim financially based on God's provision in only what He'd called us to—not on any money-making scheme I could devise. I pride myself on being an "idea person" who is extremely industrious and mostly optimistic. Getting it done, hustling it up, and making it happen—all these things are part of my nature. But I submitted my knee-jerk reaction to the Lord. I aligned my actions with the beliefs I professed to carry, and I watched myself be amazed by God and His intimate care for us.

I want to be honest and clear about this. Before we prayed and submitted to God our inclination to provide for ourselves, I was moving through my days with an integrity gap. What I professed to believe did not match up with how I lived out my faith. I said I believed that God was my provider, but I acted like whenever things got tight, I had to figure it out on my own.

Many of us—maybe all of us—don't live out what we say we believe. We live with broken, divided hearts if we don't allow God to continually hold us together. This is the cause of our dissonance—that strange suspicion that all of this isn't adding up.

This is why the songs of our lives aren't holding the same rhythm as the heart of God. We desperately want to believe these things, but our actions betray us.

- We say we depend on God, but we act like we've got to make it happen on our own.
- We say we believe God can heal, but we're walking around with decades-old wounds.
- We say we believe God is at work, but we're asleep at the wheel of this one life He's given us.

This is a point of reckoning. We are called to account.

You were created as a child deeply, impossibly loved by God. He created you with all your quirks and oddities, and He *loves* you. He *enjoys* you. He takes delight in the way you move through your days.

If we can narrow this integrity gap, we can begin to really *believe* these very good things about God's love for us. We can move that love from our heads to our hearts, and eventually we'll understand it with bone-deep assuredness. We cannot get there without looking at the integrity gap for all it is and all it's not though. I tend to believe, like a child, that if I don't acknowledge something, it will cease to exist. However, our integrity gap is there, and it will make itself known.

Scripture tells of Jesus' winnowing fork and the gathering of the wheat and burning of the chaff (Matthew 3:12)—and it's time to let the chaff be burned away in your life. I know you have bad beliefs—things that aren't serving you and certainly aren't serving the Lord. It's time to let those fall away, because if you don't, the consequences are dire.

If we believe one thing and act another way, our lives will end up having been about how we've acted rather than about how we've believed. Our actions move us, and we will end up in a far different destination than the one we believed God wanted for us.

I need you to know that closing the integrity gap cannot be carried out by anyone else. This is an inside job. It's you and your Creator, who makes things new. I'm going to do my best to empower you and equip you for renewing your mind, but you must take the action.

This is where action takes the wheel. The last thing you need are a few fluffy words for you to sleep well at night. The last thing you need is another to-do list to shine you up. The last thing you need is another Band-Aid. You don't need another voice in the echo chamber.

Here's the good news: *you already have everything you need.* God has equipped you with everything you need to close the integrity gap—obedience, embodied action, follow-through. You don't have to do it alone or without His strength, but you do have to make a choice.

Everything else in the book has led to this point. It is indicting to realize we might not be acting like we really believe what we say we believe. Our behaviors betray what we're thinking. What we think shows what we believe. The gap between the fruit in our life and the beliefs we hold shows itself here. What do we *really* believe?

It's like the fruit from the poisonous tree. Eve knew that God had said she shouldn't eat from the tree of the knowledge of good and evil (Genesis 2:17). She knew the truth with her head. But when she sank her teeth into the apple anyway, her actions were showing that while she *knew* the truth, she didn't really *believe it was true.* With her disobedient actions, she embodied a belief that God was holding out on her.

We mimic Eve every day. This is a divided heart.

INTERNAL DISSONANCE: A DIVIDED HEART

Internal dissonance shows itself as a kind of divided self. In Scripture, it's called having a heart that is "divided" (Hosea 10:2 KJV) or being "double-minded" (James 1:8), and it's a failure to fully worship the one true God. A divided heart happened in the Old Testament when people would begin to follow God but would retain some of their old religion in the wings. They'd mostly follow God or follow Him on the outside, but they wouldn't abandon their whole heart to Him. They'd keep some of their idolatrous ways—not an uncommon thing today either.

A divided heart didn't just happen in the Old Testament. Christians walk around with divided hearts every day. We've read that God will provide for us; we know it intellectually. But we have yet to actually *need* God to provide for us, so it doesn't sink into our hearts and move from knowledge to understanding. Do we really believe that God will provide for us if we've never needed Him to show us?

Even as we declare that God will protect us, we so easily worship self-made safety and comfort. We experience a profound disconnect between what we read in Scripture and what we allow ourselves to embody in obedience. We cannot know that God will protect us if we've created a world of safety at all costs. We cannot believe that God is the answer if we don't allow ourselves to need.

The Old Testament story of Elijah illustrates the challenge of a divided heart, but well before that story took place, the people of Israel had clamored for a king, thinking it would solve all their problems.

> So all the elders of Israel gathered together and came to Samuel at Ramah. They said to him, "You are old, and your

sons do not follow your ways; now appoint a king to lead us, such as all the other nations have."

But when they said, "Give us a king to lead us," this displeased Samuel; so he prayed to the LORD. And the LORD told him: "Listen to all that the people are saying to you; it is not you they have rejected, but they have rejected me as their king. As they have done from the day I brought them up out of Egypt until this day, forsaking me and serving other gods, so they are doing to you. Now listen to them; but warn them solemnly and let them know what the king who will reign over them will claim as his rights."

1 SAMUEL 8:4–9

After many generations, Ahab became the king of Israel. To put it mildly, he was not a good guy. He built a temple for Baal, married Jezebel, and made God angrier than all the previous kings of Israel combined. Now there were prophets of God in those days, and a prophet had the difficult job of speaking God's truth to people who needed to hear it. It was rarely, if ever, received well.

Here in 1 Kings 18:21, the prophet Elijah goes to the people and says, "How long will you waver between two opinions? If the LORD is God, follow him; but if Baal is God, follow him."

This is not so unimaginable today. How many of us are living with divided hearts?

I know I'm buying into a syncretistic cultural Christianity when I feel bored, frustrated, or stressed out. I'll start to believe that what Jesus said was too good to be true—lots of good ideas and interesting sayings, but none of them are actually possible or real. I'll begin to believe that for my kids to thrive, they need all the accoutrements of a wealthy, privileged childhood. I'll begin to act as though I'm the captain of my ship, hustling all the way. I'll believe that my value is in what I do, and my overflowing to-do list will be a testimony to my false beliefs.

When I live out a lethargic kind of cultural Christianity, I'm being defrauded of the richest resource in my life. I'm being tamed by the good life, the creaturely comforts, and the self-absorbed path I've set before me. I'm doing good things, moving and shaking for the kingdom. But do I even know the King?

It's possible to do good things in the name of Jesus and miss Him completely. In fact, I think it should be noted that Jesus' Sermon on the Mount warns against this high and mighty, moving and shaking, kind of life (Matthew 5–7).

These are the very real experiences of a divided heart. The dissonance we feel is real, because there is a very real disconnect between what we believe and how we're living.

It's not a "try harder" reprimand; it's a "believe better" invitation. Believe better of God and of your identity in Him. Believing better about God and your identity means that something will have to change. You won't close that gap on autopilot; it will take obedience and repentance, because a divided heart never stands for God's best.

I believe we've missed something in American Christianity— the step of obedience. We need to start walking out what we say we believe, even if we don't feel it yet. Sometimes the feelings come after the obedience, and that's okay.

Believing with your head is a great start, but God's call to us is to *keep going*! Believe with your head *and* let this belief sink deep into your heart, your hands, your feet—your whole life—as you live the very truth you believe. Let's keep going, shall we?

EXTERNAL DISSONANCE: HYPOCRISY

Most notably, living with a divided heart—where you don't really believe what you say you believe—leads to an integrity gap. This integrity gap happens because your actions—your beliefs with flesh on them—or lack thereof don't line up with what your mouth is saying.

Another way this integrity gap is defined, and this is difficult to hear, is hypocrisy. I know you don't want to think of yourself as a hypocrite—but let's revisit Paul's words in Romans 7:18–20 (MSG):

> I obviously need help! I realize that I don't have what it takes. I can will it, but I can't *do* it. I decide to do good, but I don't *really* do it; I decide not to do bad, but then I do it anyway. My decisions, such as they are, don't result in actions. Something has gone wrong deep within me and gets the better of me every time.

It "gets the better of me every time." Even when we want to do good, we can't without the Lord. And when we won't be dependent on the Lord, when we're not abiding in Him, we don't have His power or His strength. This makes it impossible to obey.

INTERNAL DISSONANCE: FRUSTRATION

Why am I not spiritually growing? Why do I feel like a fraud? I thought there was more to being a believer than this. This is the frustration that comes when the bad news in your head reigns over the good news planted in your heart. You're functionally believing a different gospel than what you say you believe.

The frustration comes from a lack of integrity, a lack of wholeness. Your soul isn't in agreement about which way you're going. You're headed in two different directions, and it's no wonder you're feeling like you're just running in place. You're exhausted, fed up, and ready to quit.

EXTERNAL DISSONANCE: HIDING IN SHAME

Eventually, this frustration will lead to despair, to feeling like there's no point at all. This is the natural end of trying your hardest at something you'll never be able to do. And to be clear, we cannot obey God outside of the Spirit's strength, because obeying God requires a whole heart. He demands our total surrender.

But listen. Repentance brings refreshment.

The other day, our oldest son was about five minutes late getting home. He'd ridden his bike to a friend's house, and it was further away than we'd ever let him ride before. Mike and I were both a little hesitant to let him go, but we're trying to let him grow in independence. We're also trying to grow in dependence on the Lord as we parent Noah with wider fences.

Noah is an exceptionally obedient child. This is not from anything we've done—I won't be writing a parenting book anytime soon! This is purely how the Lord made him, and I imagine it's partly due to his birth order positioning as the oldest of four boys. He's the straight and narrow, the good soldier, the one you never have to worry about.

But he was five minutes late on this first test of a new, widened boundary. We hardly ever have to discipline him, because he is so disciplined himself. And when Mike told him that he'd fallen short of our expectation, Noah crumbled. As the oldest daughter in my family, I remember that feeling and still struggle with it. Letting down people I love hurts so bad, and I think it's because of how much of my identity can come from being the one who always does well. When I don't do well, I shock myself.

Noah did not want to apologize to Mike. He curled up on the couch and buried his head in shame. I didn't want that for Noah; Mike didn't want that for Noah. But this is how he was choosing to deal with his disobedience. He was hiding.

Adam and Eve hid. Noah hid. I hide all the time.

But like I told Noah the other night, repentance leads to refreshment. I know that repentance can be a very "churchy" word, but all I really mean here is coming to the Lord and admitting that you've turned away from Him and His best and have selfishly gone your own way. Then you just turn back toward Him, and He'll welcome you back with joy. He will fill your cup again as you rest in the acceptance that you didn't earn.

When we fall short, we often hide in shame from God, from others, and from ourselves. But this book is about shining light on the mess in your head and asking God to come into it. He wants to clear out the cobwebs and replace your self-manufactured bad news with the good news of Jesus.

There is great hope. You are going to be restored. There is an ancient practice that believers through generations have tried and tested, and we'll look at it in the next chapter.

PART THREE

Preach to Yourself

CHAPTER NINE

God Gives Us a Better Way

The LORD your God is in your midst,
 a mighty one who will save;
he will rejoice over you with gladness;
 he will quiet you by his love;
he will exult over you with loud singing.

ZEPHANIAH 3:17 ESV

I'm afraid I'm going to lose you here. I'm going to talk about a superhero movie. I have to say that I'm *not* a superhero movie kind of girl. I don't like science fiction, and I'm not interested in techy types of fantasy movies either. I don't like dystopian movies. I like my movies firmly grounded in reality, please, and thank you so very much.

But I couldn't stay away from this one. I saw *Wonder Woman* this year, and I admit that I was one of those women silently weeping in the movie theater. I was entranced by the depiction of a powerful, wise, and confident woman. I also loved that a woman directed the movie, and I think you could really tell from a filmmaking perspective. I walked out holding Mike's hand and mourning that we didn't have daughters to raise to be brave and strong like a superhero. I also started thinking about how I could pass legislation that required every girl to see that movie when they turn fourteen. I was in full-fledged, unapologetic, unabashed girl-power mode.

Because I haven't quite quit the girl-power feeling, I imagine you right there inside the movie. You're like my super heroine. I love you, and I believe in you. I see your superpowers more than you do, because I have a wider view than other audience members. We've reached the middle of the movie. You're looking a little worse for wear. You are worn-out, busted, and bruised. You've expended all your energy, and you've done all you know to do.

You've hit that point in the movie when you're realizing that your worst enemy isn't the foe you're fighting externally; it's *yourself.*

It's not easy to hear all the ways we've been filling our minds with bad news. All the ways we've been working against ourselves when we're only trying to be strong. But here we are. We've stared ourselves down—and seeing our sin (or to put it more simply, seeing where we fall short) always has this effect. We get weak-kneed, and it takes our breath away. If we're not enough now, how can we possibly keep going?

But our heroine never stays there for long. This is the moment when you're flat on the ground and the viewer fears you're not going to get up. This blow has been the hit to take you down.

And then, the moment of resurrection. Our heroine (you!) opens one eye when we thought she was dead. The moviegoers are filled with a swell of hope. We feel powerful on her behalf. We know she's faced her worst critic, her worst enemy, her worst nightmare.

This is the turning point in the movie when it's all power from here. The music crescendos to a powerful roar. The film pace slows so we catch every single detail. We know now that our heroine is going to win this battle. Cue the tears—my tears, if we're keeping score.

As little as I like superhero movies, I believe this much in you. I am over here cheering you on, trying to keep myself from asking Zondervan to put a QR code to my favorite *Wonder Woman* scene right here for a morale boost. I believe you are far stronger than you know, because you have the Spirit of the living God nestled deep inside you. That is something that can never be shaken loose.

Our minds, our brains, practically have superpowers too. Our brains are able to grow and change as we have new and different experiences in life. Our experiences literally prompt our brains to change shape. When we are aware of our thoughts and change them, we light up our brains' wiring. When we activate our minds in this way, we can strengthen the "synaptic linkages."[1]

There is literally a way to change our minds. It's what Scripture refers to in Romans 12:1–2, where we're called to renew our minds.

> Therefore, I urge you, brothers and sisters, in view of God's mercy, to offer your bodies as a living sacrifice, holy and pleasing to God—this is your true and proper worship. Do not conform to the pattern of this world, but be transformed by the renewing of your mind. Then you will be able to test and approve what God's will is—his good, pleasing and perfect will.

God created our bodies with a brain that is able to grow and change. This is shockingly good news. Even before science could confirm it, Christians for millennia had the ability to mold and form their minds to be like Christ's. Now we have science to back up what Scripture has always claimed to be true. We will be transformed, made new, when we renew our minds.

We renew our minds, and God transforms us. That's what Romans 12:2 promises. Romans 12:2 is an if-then statement. If we renew our minds, then God will make us into something new.

But how do we do that?

There was a time when I had a pretty dead spiritual life. It looked fine from the outside, because I had long ago become adept at putting on a show. I knew what people were looking for in a successful Christian leader, and I emulated that. It wasn't that I was living in defiant sin, but I was absolutely not living in abundance.

I was not experiencing growth, and it seemed impossible that God could do a new thing in my life.

When I read the Word, it felt like I'd read it all a million times before. There didn't seem to be anything new or alive or active about the Bible. When I prayed, I felt like I was just putting in my time. When I was quiet, I was only bored. When I was still, I was restless. I was far from spiritually healthy, and I wasn't bearing much real fruit.

I believed that God forgave me for the sins I committed before I was a Christian, but from there, I felt like I was on my own. I was living in my own self-imposed, "pull yourself up by the bootstraps" religion. I had some fundamentally wrong beliefs about God, and they eventually came out in my actions.

I was exhausted. I was bored. I was unimpressed. I was tired of trying to be good, and I was irate when good things happened to bad people. I was constantly nervous that the bottom was going to fall out of my mostly perfect life.

But God changed my heart.

This is why I write, and this is why I'll always believe in the power of good books about God and His Word. When I read Emily Freeman's *Grace for the Good Girl*, it was like something deep within me shifted. I'd been struggling with exhaustion in the Christian life and constant annoyance that no one else was even trying to be good and therefore weren't as exhausted as I was. I was as graceless as that sounds, and I'm sure I was a real joy to be around.

Then I read, "When we believe that God expects us to try hard to become who Jesus wants us to be, we will live in that blurry, frustrating land of Should Be rather than trust in The One Who Is."[2] And, "But understand that the reason it is so difficult to extend forgiveness to those who have failed us is because *we are unable to receive forgiveness for our own failures.*"[3]

For some reason, Emily's words helped make things click for me. I was trying to be good in my own strength for Jesus, absolutely convinced that it's what the Christian life is all about. However, I couldn't have missed it more if I was missing on purpose. This revelation didn't mean I believed in Jesus for the first time; in fact, I'd been following Him for more than a decade. But I began to believe that I didn't have to keep it all so impeccably pulled together.

Previously, I had believed that Jesus had saved me from my past sin, my past stupidity, my past indiscretions. But I also believed that He was staring at me like a frustrated parent, chiding me about how this was my "last chance." He had given me all the grace He had to give, and from the point of conversion on, it was up to me to be good.

You can imagine how I walked around like I was on a tightrope, frustrated and fists clenched. I didn't want to disappoint my Father, especially when my "second chance" had already come to pass at salvation and I was pretty sure He wasn't giving out third chances.

But He does! And what's even better is that His Spirit gives us the power to grow, transform, and live fully when we open our hearts in obedience to Him. When I finally understood the gospel—that it was for me and was for every single day—it changed everything. I started accepting God's forgiveness over and over, and this changed me even more. When I started living as though I was forgiven, I believed that God was infinitely better than I'd imagined. He hadn't forgiven me just of what I didn't know better, but of what I *did* know better.

To keep the gospel at the top of my mind, I started preaching to myself. I would quote Scripture:

- "Therefore, there is now no condemnation for those who are in Christ Jesus" (Romans 8:1).
- "Here is a trustworthy saying that deserves full acceptance: Christ Jesus came into the world to save sinners—of whom I am the worst" (1 Timothy 1:15).
- "For my yoke is easy and my burden is light" (Matthew 11:30).

When I believed that God wasn't good, I told myself He most certainly was. When I believed that I wasn't forgiven, I remembered that I was. When I told myself I couldn't do it anymore, I reminded myself that God said I could do all things through Christ.

I just began to tell myself the good news of Jesus over and over, and it began to stick. When I caught myself listening to or repeating bad news to myself, I immediately countered it with what I knew to be true. My false belief of choice is, unfortunately, "I can't do this." And every time I catch myself—and I still catch myself saying this—I make note of it and then add "without You" at the end.

So "I can't do this" becomes "I can't do this *without You*," which I derive from the apostle Paul's declaration that he can do all things in God's strength (Philippians 4:13). I began to see changes in the way my mind was wired, and over time, that power sank into the deepest recesses of my heart.

This is how we talk back with truth. This is how we renew our minds.

In the morning when my alarm went off and my first inclination was to groan, "I can't do this," I would say, "I can't do this *without You*," as a reminder to simply abide in the Lord. Or if I was feeling particularly chipper and optimistic, I'd reply "I can do anything with You, Lord." And I would continue this refrain throughout my day, in the face of every nuisance or inconvenience—things like losing important files on my computer and a child vomiting in the middle of the night. I can definitely endure those things with Christ by my side.

In order to best believe the good news, we need to clear the bad news out. The bad news I was believing when my spirituality was lifeless was that God had forgiven me for my past but I was in charge of being perfect from here on out.

That bad news manifested itself in so many areas of my life.

I was worn-out from performing. And since I'd become so used to performing well, *everything* started to feel like a performance. It mattered more how my spiritual life appeared than how healthy it really was. And because I felt as though I was exhausting myself in trying to perform well, I was graceless with and annoyed at anyone else who didn't seem to be performing as well. Talk about a no-good, bad-news antigospel, huh?

None of this was malicious, and at the time, I wouldn't have been able to diagnose it as the issue. But by God's gift of hindsight, I can see clearly that this bad news I was believing was a lie planted by Satan to keep me from delighting in God's good gift of grace. I wholly misunderstood grace, and it killed my intimacy with the Lord and therefore the fruit of my spiritual life.

But if we can recognize the bad news we're believing, we've got a shot at renewing our minds! That's great news. And the especially helpful news is that there's an ancient biblical way to retrain your brain, which we'll explore together.

STEP 1: CALL OUT FALSE BELIEFS

We sleuth out bad news lies like it's our job. What are we believing that just isn't true? To do this well, we're going to have to get quiet and listen to the Lord. We'll need to abide in Him, realizing that we've reached the end of our ability to make it work on our own. We need to watch what He's already doing in our lives so we can be spiritually aware and join with Him.

It would also be helpful to look at your wounds. What are the really tender things that have been said to you or have happened to you? As you examine the wounds, you'll be able to see if any false beliefs have sprung up.

This can be the most time-consuming part of the challenge, because we aren't always aware when we're believing something that just isn't true. It sounds like truth to us, because it's often in our own voice. So don't be frustrated if it seems difficult to figure this part out. Ask God to illuminate it for you. I always want to skip that part—the asking God part. It seems ineffectual and inefficient, and if I'm honest about one of *my* false beliefs, I'm prone to believe I'll figure it out on my own eventually. But lately I've begun praying fervently about things that confuse me or are unclear, and God's been good to bring clarity where there was none. And it has the amazing side effect of making me feel so loved and seen by God. I believe Him in such new and profound ways because He feels so near. When God gets in your head, you know you've gotten really close to Him.

Author Macy Halford spoke recently about how before God brought light to creation, it was full of chaos and confusion.[4] It was dark and unformed, but once God separated dark from light and gave things names, He began to call things good. We must go deep into the dark recesses of our minds and pull these false beliefs out, tackle them to the ground, and get a good look at them. We take the bad news at face value, learn what it sounds like, and try to tease out what it looks like when we believe it.

STEP 2: TAKE THOUGHTS CAPTIVE AND CALL THEM BY NAME

This part will seem simple, but beware: it's the repetition that can get difficult. It can feel like you're going to be chasing after your own thoughts all day every day. And to be fair, this is true at the beginning.

After we've identified a false belief, we need to listen for it in our thoughts and speech. We need to see how we're believing it and look at the fruit it's bearing in our life. As I said earlier, my most prevalent false belief is, "I can't do it." It stops me before I get started. It's a very clever tactic of the Enemy, because once I get an idea in my head and believe I can do it, I'm unstoppable. But if Satan makes me question my abilities or the goodness of something in the first place, I will just crawl back into bed (sometimes figuratively, but many times literally) in defeat.

But now we know what our false belief sounds like. Maybe yours is, "Things are never going to change." You've had the courage to wade into the dark and wrangle this bad belief into the light. Praise God! Truly. Wrangling ideas in your mind is difficult and tiring work. That kind of adventure can get you dark and twisty quickly. But now we see the false belief and can call it what it is. We can put a name to it. It's a false belief of futility versus fruitfulness. Do you have the ability to bear fruit? That's what you really don't believe. You don't believe you have the ability to bear fruit—or rather, that God does not have the power to bear fruit through you.

STEP 3: REPLACE FALSE BELIEFS WITH TRUTH AND DEVELOP NEW PATHS

When we hear ourselves playing a bad news loop, we stop it right away. Then we put something better on. We replace it with truth. And once we do that, we can begin to wear new paths in our brains. We stay on that new and narrow path. We refuse to veer back onto the well-worn path of false belief.

It sounds simplistic, and maybe it sounds too good to be true. Maybe you've lived for many years with a powerless, frustrated faith that has always left you wanting. Maybe you feel like a total fraud, and you're about ready to give up on this faith thing altogether. None of it is working out like you thought it would. Your life change just isn't happening.

I've found that sometimes we have to preach ourselves out of a mess. We sometimes start in a hole and have to partner with God; we must trust Him again before we start to see any big difference. But once we begin the practice of renewing our minds, He comes through and makes us more like Christ.

And then again, we preach to ourselves when life is easy, paving the way for us to prepare for the times when things aren't easy. This is real life in a hard, fallen world. We experience the consequences of our sins and the sins of others every day. We deal with the sickness that invaded right after Adam and Eve were kicked out of the garden for good. We mourn the effects of sin and death and broken relationships. It's all profoundly heartbreaking and can be too much at times.

But when we fix our minds on Christ, when we lean on the living leadership of the Holy Spirit, we are able to endure and renew our minds, and He makes us something altogether different.

> The Spirit searches all things, even the deep things of God. For who knows a person's thoughts except their own spirit within them? In the same way no one knows the thoughts of God except the Spirit of God. What we have received is not the spirit of the world, but the Spirit who is from God, so that we may understand what God has freely given us. This is what we speak, not in words taught us by human wisdom but in words taught by the Spirit, explaining spiritual realities with Spirit-taught words. The person without the Spirit does not accept the things that come from the Spirit of God but considers them foolishness, and cannot understand them because they are discerned only through the Spirit. The person with the Spirit makes judgments about all things, but such a person is not subject to merely human judgments, for,
>
> "Who has known the mind of the Lord
> so as to instruct him?"
>
> *But we have the mind of Christ.*
>
> 1 CORINTHIANS 2:10–16,
> EMPHASIS ADDED

This truth knocks me back a bit. It seems impossible. How can I have the mind of Christ? Sometimes my mind feels chaotic and confusing, dark and twisty. If nothing else, most of the time it just feels busy. Those are not the ways of the Lord, so how is it possible that I have the mind of Christ?

In the passage from 1 Corinthians 2, Paul implies that the Spirit is as intimately entwined with God as our own mind is with ourselves. Our mind *is* ourselves.[5] Just as we cannot know what's in another person's mind until they communicate it to us, we cannot know what is in the mind of God until it is communicated to us. We have the mind of Christ—which seems impossible—because the Spirit who is also in us communicates it to us.

Because we can know the mind of Christ, we take hold of the mind of Christ and obey the mind of Christ. With the power of the Spirit, we can discern spiritual things and lay down our false beliefs.

You and I are not stuck in our own chaotic minds. We have the mind of Christ, which is *very* good news indeed!

CHAPTER TEN

Stop and Listen to Yourself

In my own life I've found it to be true that when I hold on to the wrong things, the wrong things hold on to me.

EMILY P. FREEMAN, *SIMPLY TUESDAY*

*M*y friend Lara hosts a workshop in Chapel Hill, North Carolina, called "Making Things Happen." I went one year, totally not knowing what to expect. Having heard from past attendees, I knew it was powerful, but I also knew they took your cell phones and encouraged you to stay unplugged all weekend. There was no other information available—and as an amateur internet super-sleuth, you can be sure I looked high and low. You almost got the feeling that it was secretive on purpose.

The weekend *was* life-changing, but one of the most powerful exercises had Lara asking us to lie on our backs on the floor with our feet out in front of us. She asked us to close our eyes and listen to her voice.

We were supposed to imagine being eighty years old. We were surrounded by our loved ones, reminiscing about our life. We were supposed to think of what they were saying to us, about what things they were glad we had done. We were supposed to look around and see who was there, what we were surrounded by, and what actual dwelling we found ourselves in. The point was to look at things from a perspective that was outside of our current pace of life and get almost a godlike view of our life. This visual exercise led me to some of the most clarity I've ever had regarding my purpose and how I want to spend my time.

I want to walk you through a similar exercise. This will help you recognize the bad news you're telling yourself. My hope is that you'll learn about yourself in a real aha-moment sort of way. But you'll also need to learn to recognize the loops in the day in, day out of your life. You'll need to bridge from that knowledge to understanding through lived action.

A quarterback will watch game tape and be able to spot defenses that other teams run. He'll be able to get a glimpse of the big picture of how the opponent works. This is the aha, the one moment in time. But then the quarterback will also have to get into the game and recognize in the heat of the moment, in real time, those same defenses he saw in the video. Both are valuable experiences, and both are needed. In this exercise, you'll have a learning moment, and then you'll also see it in action in your day-to-day life.

Maybe you already know the bad news that cycles through your day. Some people are just hyperaware of their thoughts. But sometimes our own voices can drone on and become so comfortable and familiar that we lose the ability to really discern what we're saying to ourselves and hearing from others.

Here are a few ways to do the work of recognizing the bad loops you're embracing.

1. Imagine your worst morning. This is the kind of morning where you sleep through the alarm and are late for work or an appointment. As you hop out of bed, you bump your knee on the side of your bed. You burn your tongue on the hot coffee you're trying to slurp down so the caffeine kicks in and you wake up. We've all had those mornings. These are the kinds of mornings where it feels like absolutely nothing is going your way. Everything you try fails. Every single thing you do to salvage the situation only makes it worse.

2. Ask yourself what is running through your head (or out of your mouth) during this mundanely awful kind of morning?

Is it condemnation of yourself for not being more responsible and setting two alarms? Is it condemnation of other people for your circumstances—maybe your husband pressed snooze on your alarm or your roommate left something on the floor that you tripped over? Are you believing you deserve this kind of morning because you can never get your act together? Are you sure that nothing is ever going to change? What phrase do you say over and over as each annoyingly, frustratingly normal thing goes wrong?

3. Write that phrase down. Do you have a list? Think about it, pray about it, and if this all seems too abstract, wait until you have another one of those mornings (and we all know they're more common than we want them to be!).

4. Leave that scene behind. Imagine you got through the day and things got better, but the day was normal in all other aspects. It was just a regular kind of day. You've lived thousands of them before. You've come home and done your normal evening routine. You're not up, and you're not down. This is one of those nights when life is just steady. You crawl into bed and your head hits the pillow. You settle in and replay the scenes of the day against the shadows of your closed eyes. What are you cataloging? What are you dwelling on as you drift off to sleep?

These are some of the quietest moments of the day, and what you think about during these times is often telling. Are you thinking about the way you let your mom down? Are you beating yourself up for an awkward conversation with someone you're trying to love well? Are you plotting for an unknown future, pulling the strings on what life could end up like for you? Are you mentally counting the dollars that your bank account does or doesn't hold?

If you've had a hard time imagining these moments, this one is really the kicker. Pay attention here. There are times in life that fall under the category of what is called "fight or flight." You're faced with a decision, and you either back out or you stay and grind it out. These are the times when you learn what you're made of.

Think to some of your most recent fight-or-flight moments. Maybe you were faced with an impossible task at work or you had to tell someone some really bad news. Maybe your bank account ran dry before the end of the month for yet another month. I want you to examine these times and see what your mind is made of. Are you full to the gills with bad news echoing off the walls of your skull? What is whispering between your ears?

I think we're all predisposed to having not so awesome times of the day. Nights are particularly bad for me. There is something about the house being quiet and there's no real work to be done, and now I'm left to myself. We have a personal marriage rule that we don't have any serious discussions or make any big decisions after ten at night. It's just too late for my mind to think rationally. I get upset more easily, misunderstand Mike's intentions, and spin stories that are most likely false.

Leaving me to myself is not always the best idea, but I've come to learn that quieting myself is an important spiritual discipline. Gone are the days when I thought it was healthy to do the whole "stuff and distract" thing. It's important to take an honest look at your thoughts. Nothing will change without first being recognized.

5. Look your bad news in the face and talk back with truth. This bad news is the "truth" you're telling yourself; it's the "truth" you're believing. Take a long look. Read it like a headline. This is the story of your life, because it's the life of your mind. Then make the choice, with Christ as your companion, to change the story—moment by moment, thought by thought.

I came across a short, powerful video of Abi Stumvoll, who lives in Redding, California. She's a blonde, spitfire kind of young woman who paces around the stage like she's on a mission. Abi describes how from the time she was seven years old on, she would think, *I want to die.* This is shocking, because a seven-year-old seems so tiny and tender. I know because I tuck a seven-year-old little boy into bed every night. He still has that little-kid, delicate swoop of a nose and those still pudgy little hands. It's hard to imagine such dark thoughts flowing through a child's head.

It's also shocking because Abi is a pastor. We are wrong if we believe we're the only ones who cycle through these lies. Every person in every walk of life, every profession, and every town struggles to get their mind to obey their spirit. This is the human condition. Abi overcame her repetitive cycle of bad news the same way we all have to, and the first step is to recognize what it is that we're hearing over and over.

When I first heard that Abi's knee-jerk thought to *everything* was *I want to die*, I could feel something click to life in my brain. It struck me that as long as I can remember, my go-to silent reaction to every single thing that went wrong has been, *I can't do this.*

If I have my arms full and drop something, I think . . . *I can't do this.*

If my four-year-old wakes me up for a drink of water in the middle of the night, I think . . . *I can't do this.*

If I let someone down and have to ask them for forgiveness, I think . . . *I can't do this.*

It's my go-to, knee-jerk, first-blush answer to almost everything negative, inconvenient, or frustrating in my life. I intellectually know I *can* do almost anything, and Scripture says I can do *all things* through Jesus, who gives me strength. So it struck me like a right hook to the jaw when I realized that I think, *I can't do this*, at least twenty times a day.

Why am I telling myself this lie? Why do I repeat it over and over? If I dig deeper, I think the answer is, *I don't* want *to do this*. And that might be getting closer to my true beliefs.

I can't do this. Why would I tell myself that?

"I can do all this through him who gives me strength" (Philippians 4:13). This is the good news of my soul. This is what I know in my bones. So why in the world do I tell myself such bad news? My repeated thought isn't even, *I don't* think *I can do this*. That would at least open it up for discussion and persuasion, encouragement and a "you can do it!" No, this is simply, *I can't do this*. Case closed, over and out, done and done. It's like I don't even want to fight.

But I *have* to fight. I have to hear what I'm repeating. I have to look the bad news straight on and take note. I have to jot that thought down and ask God why it is that I think it so often. Why is this important to me? How has it gotten lodged into my inner conversation?

How do you react when your day goes sideways or you don't get what you want? What are your knee-jerk, first-blush thoughts when you get bad news or compare yourself to others? When you're at the end of yourself, what is the first thing that pops into your head?

Maybe you're like me and you think, *I can't do this.*

This is a false belief about capacity or power. Other versions of this might sound like, *I can't handle this* or *I'm going to fail* or *I'm not cut out for this* or *Why can't I do this?*

Maybe at the end of your rope you realize that you're just not enough.

This is bad news you're telling yourself about your soul's identity and security. These lies might be more like, *I'm a mess* or *There's something wrong with me* or *I don't make a difference* or *No one cares about me.* Maybe you mutter, *Nothing is ever going to change.*

This is the wrongheaded idea that there is no hope or that things are futile. I look for words like *never, ever,* and *always* to discern these false beliefs in others. They may sound like, *I will never change* or *I already messed up, so I may as well quit* or *Everything good in my life has already happened.*

These false beliefs may look frightening when we see them spelled out in black and white, but we may as well bring them into the light. We must keep dragging them to the light. I promise, I did not like looking the lie of *I can't do this* head-on, but when I did, I was able to begin to steer my mind in the right direction.

I believe that things can change, because creating, re-creating, renewing—these are all parts of the very nature of God. He makes things out of nothing. He sends a baby to save the world—not a fully grown adult, but a baby who is going to grow and change and learn throughout life. He gives us the Spirit to illuminate *His very own thoughts* for us! Why would He do that if we couldn't align ourselves with Him? He made us with the ability to change, and He gave us His Spirit to equip us with the power to change. Our brains are pliable and adaptable organs. We have the ability to change our minds! I cannot wait to see the way the world changes when a whole generation of women begin to change their minds.

CHAPTER ELEVEN

The Good Work of Turning Around

Every time you make a choice you are turning the central part of you, the part of you that chooses, into something a little different from what it was before. And taking your life as a whole, with all your innumerable choices, all your life long you are slowly turning this central thing either into a heavenly creature or into a hellish creature: either into a creature that is in harmony with God, and with other creatures, and with itself, or else into one that is in a state of war and hatred with God, and with its fellow-creatures, and with itself . . . Each of us at each moment is progressing to one state or the other.

C. S. LEWIS, *MERE CHRISTIANITY*

*M*y oldest son Noah called to me from the shower. He had forgotten to bring a towel into the bathroom, and now he was dripping wet, freezing, and perched on the edge of the tub. I pulled myself out from under the cozy covers and padded down the hall to the linen closet, crossing my fingers that we had clean towels. It was the end of a harried week for our family, and I'd been finding that most things in our house were dirty.

Of course, there were no clean towels in the closet, so I marched to the bathroom door and scolded Noah for getting into the shower without having a towel handy. I was already thinking, *I can't do this*, with regard to the entirety of the day ahead if this is the way it was starting.

At that same moment, I heard Asher, who is my most independent child, rummaging through a high cabinet in the kitchen. There was next to no reason for him to be in the cabinet, and as I made my way downstairs and into the kitchen, I saw him standing on his tiptoes on the counter, reaching for a mixing bowl.

"We're out of cereal bowls," he said with the sweetest, most apologetic look. I felt like I'd failed him, and it was about enough to put me over the edge and back into bed for the morning.

I headed back upstairs to get some consolation from my husband, Mike, and I was greeted by a panicked look that told me he was out of either socks or underwear. Today it was very possibly both.

I can't do this. I can't do this. I can't do this. The pitter-patter of false belief paced through my mind. It wasn't that anything terribly awful had happened, but I didn't get to start my morning before already feeling horribly behind. The mornings in our house are my domain, and it's my job to make sure everyone has what they need to get a good start to the day. And today I had failed.

Once I got the kids on the bus, I realized I didn't have enough gas to make it to the office and didn't have enough time to stop to fill up. *I can't do this.* I spilled my coffee on my lap, necessitating a rapid-fire outfit change. *I cannot do this. I can't do it today.*

Before I even got into the office, I had expended great amounts of mental energy telling myself I couldn't do something that was clearly already in motion. My false belief was that I couldn't do it, but the reality of the situation was that I could and I was—even if it didn't feel like it was going great.

Have you ever had one of those days when you just can't turn it around? Every little thing that can go wrong does, and you have a sour attitude to match? On days that like, I can feel the weird little tickle of aggression sneak up on me. It's almost like I need to go run a mile just to get that offensive energy out. Once a day like that gets going, it's incredibly hard for me to change directions.

Instead of just choosing correctly and making a change, I normally have to totally stop in my tracks. I have to do something to shift the momentum of the situation. I have to pull to a complete stop—throw on my brakes, perform the whole rollback. I have to keep my energy from moving forward in an unhealthy direction.

This is difficult to do. Newton's first law of motion tells us that once an object is in motion, it will keep moving unless it is acted on by another force. If we allow our minds to keep chattering false beliefs to us, we're likely to continue to believe them. It takes work and energy to stop the false beliefs in their tracks.

Remember how your brain works? You have billions of neurons that each fire every time you have a thought. Your neurons make connections with each other and form bonds and patterns over time. You've gotten into a rut with the patterns of your thoughts to this point.

Your brain has a small, seahorse-shaped part called the hippocampus. *Hippocampus* means "seahorse" in Latin, which seems like an elementary classifying system when we speak of such a complex organ. Alas, this tiny, seahorse-shaped region of your brain is responsible for your emotions and, in part, for your motivation. The hippocampus is chock-full of granule cells, which are one of the few neurons that the brain can generate more of. When a new neuron is formed, this is called neurogenesis. Neuroplasticity is the way these neurons connect with each other to form new pathways. There's a lot going on in this little seahorse!

In January 2017, scientists at the University of Alabama at Birmingham found that it was possible for the brain to create brand-new neurons that wove themselves into existing neural circuits, allowing the synaptic connections to grow stronger and heartier. The old neurons would die off when the new, stronger connections were formed.[1] You can't just count on time to break down the connections in your brain; you need to actively retrain your mind to make new connections. Otherwise, you'll simply be reinforcing the old neural pathways.

And here we find great hope. In order to move forward in something new and different, we need to renew our minds. To do that, our minds need a new connection.

Repentance can feel like a heavy word. Maybe it's a new word altogether for you. But repentance is the way God uses to change us. Let me show you what I mean.

When we recognize our bad news, it is a watershed moment. Hopefully you've been digging deep and asking God to reveal what is playing on repeat. It may take days or weeks, but I hope a pattern emerges to you. I hope you're able to write down those thoughts or tell them to a friend, so you'll be more apt to snatch them out of space when you think them.

When you realized the junk you were preaching to yourself, I hope you took your heavy heart to God in sorrow and asked Him to change your mind—which is what repentance is about. We really can do that! It may feel foreign to do, but we pray for physical healing from things like cancer or injuries we've suffered in an accident. We clearly believe that God can work at a cellular level.

When we feel frustrated or stuck in our ruts of false belief, we can pray that God will change the very neural pathways in our brain. We can ask Him to rewire the innermost parts of our minds on a biological level. He created us. He knit us together in our mothers' bellies. I believe that He can change the way my brain tangles together and makes connections. Do you believe that too?

Let's practice together. We can pray this prayer when we're feeling the effects of our false beliefs:

Lord, You are mighty in me. You made me. You put every cell together and came up with me. You are the Lord of my life, and You are the Lord of my mind. Lord, I have believed things that are not true, and I'm sorry for that. Please forgive me. Lord, because You are good, would You let the ways I used to think die off and then would You blaze a new trail in my mind? Would You stop connections in my brain that are tied to my old way of thinking and form new neural pathways with Your good truth? Thank You, Lord, for Your forgiveness

*and for the miraculous way You made me. Please remake my
mind to be more like Yours.*

That is a beautiful moment of repentance—of receiving His
grace that comes after we go to Him, humble, needy, unable to
heal ourselves.

That is one moment of repentance—repentance for years of
being a false preacher in your own head, repentance for overlook-
ing His good news and still preferring the bad news. This is the
kind of repenting that happens a thousand times a day. When
you go about your day and all is well, you thank God for keeping
you on the narrow path. When you catch a bad news loop gearing
up, you shush it, preach to yourself, and then get back to the good
news. You pray, "Forgive me, God. I *want* to believe; please help
me overcome my unbelief."

This is the kind of repentance where you skin your knees and
get back up. This is the kind of repentance that you commit to,
knowing that God is urging you on to good works. His Spirit is
mighty in you, and you are renewing your mind!

Don't get stuck in guilt and shame. The work of turning
around is the work of honesty and wholeness. There is a peaceful kind of power that comes when you go God's way, however
imperfectly it might be.

In Romans 12:2, the apostle Paul writes, "Do not conform to
the pattern of this world, but be transformed by the renewing of
your mind." You renew; God transforms. To "be transformed"
means that something outside of you is doing the transforming.
You must be faithful to take the thoughts captive, but ultimately,
God is the only one who can change our minds.

CHAPTER TWELVE

Cutting New Paths and Taking New Ground

A dead thing can go with the stream, but only a living thing can go against it.

G. K. CHESTERTON,
THE EVERLASTING MAN

*H*ave you ever seen a gymnast compete? They are compact little dynamos of explosive power. They have the balance that allows them to soar through the air and land squarely on a four-inch-wide piece of wood suspended four feet off the ground. They have the strength to hurl themselves over the vault, landing perfectly in complete stillness when done correctly. And I haven't even mentioned the flexibility, precision, and mental courage that are required.

We gain our best attributes when we push and pull against something. We become stronger and more competent, ready for whatever is asked. God has already equipped us with what we need to get stronger; we just need to engage. Once we stop our momentum, we can easily get turned around and head in the wrong direction. We need to wear new paths.

This is where it gets hard for me. It's routine. It takes discipline. It's unglamorous, and there are no people cheering you on around every corner. This is the dirty work of renewing your mind. You are cocreating with God in blazing new trails in your brain. You're like a pioneer in a covered wagon. The landscape is going to look foreign, and you'll be unacquainted with your mental surroundings. But you're heading somewhere good.

I'm pretty good at the big moments. The breakthroughs. The bravado. But the follow-through—the slow and steady maintenance that comes afterward—that's a whole other animal. I don't want to do the work after the energy of the epiphany has faded away back to normal. I don't want to do the work when I'm alone and no one is watching. But that's the definition I've always heard of integrity. It's the person we are when no one is watching. And we're looking for wholeness here. We're looking for our thought life to line up with our beliefs.

If you're the kind of person who needs a little bravado to motivate you, think of it this way. This is the wild wild West of your mind, and you're going to tame it. You're staring at the uncharted mess of your thoughts, and you're bringing them under control.

You're going to go out every day and chop down trees. You're going to smash the bad news out of the way, and you're going to make a clearing. You're going to build your own little log cabin near the stream of Living Water, and you're going to drink from that cool, clean water every single day. Whenever you're tempted to go back, you need to remember that there is glory here. You are taking new ground, and you are *not* going back. This is the way of the Lord.

Philippians 3:13–14 reads, "Brothers and sisters, I do not consider myself yet to have taken hold of it. But one thing I do: Forgetting what is behind and straining toward what is ahead, I press on toward the goal to win the prize for which God has called me heavenward in Christ Jesus."

It's going to feel like wilderness at first—it's off the beaten path. At the beginning it can feel like an adventure—challenging and unpredictable—but I'm gonna do it, by golly.

After Eli was born four years ago, I wanted to try the new health fad circulating among my friends and on Instagram. You may have done it yourself. If so, hats off to you! I embarked on the Whole30 program, and I was set up for success. I cleaned out our pantry, eliminating all glorious (and awful, according to Whole30!) Pop-Tarts, pasta, and prepackaged convenience food. I sauntered through the aptly named Whole Foods and filled my cart with all manner of expensive "Whole30-compliant" thises and thats.

I was ready to go, and while I'd never had a good experience with an "all or nothing" kind of plan, I felt optimistic. I felt like I could do hard things, like a trailblazer would do. It felt full of fun possibilities—until I got into it. Then it got hard. I had to change nearly every way I had ever eaten. I had to make foods from scratch while my toddlers pulled at the ankles of my pants. Every single thing was difficult, and I was doing it without caffeine, sugar, or white flour. It felt nearly impossible.

I completed what I now call my Whole36Hours when I called Mike at work, wracked with sobs while lying on the ground from what I can only imagine was a hormonal carb crash. Everything was working against me as I tried to change my lifestyle regarding food. I was time crunched because I was raising four boys. I was exhausted because I was also working. I was hormonal because I had an infant. And now they were trying to take my carbs away from me.

Looking back, I think I would have been more successful under different circumstances. I know I'd change a couple things for sure. First, I'd do it in community. I'd have a herd of friends doing Whole30 alongside me. I know that Whole30 is ultimately an individual sport (much like preaching to yourself), but knowing that others were journeying the hard road with me would have made a big difference.

Second, I would have read more about what to expect during the month-long project. I know the originators of Whole30 produced a guide specifically with that in mind. They lay out what to expect during each day of the process. They warn of when you'll feel a sugar crash and when you'll want to give up, and they'll tell you when it will start to get easier.

My friend Jess and I had a little code we used when we'd been dwelling on the bad news for a little too long, when we knew we needed to pull up from the sinking feeling and thoughts we were having and rest, floating on the surface of what we knew to be true. That's the beauty of truth—it's vast enough to hold us up. All we have to do is come to it.

Sometimes Jess and I were able to buoy ourselves with truth we had memorized and integrated into our lives so much that it was in our bones. Other times, we needed to buoy each other. This is the beauty of the body of Christ. We don't have to struggle against lies by ourselves. We are our sisters' keepers. We have the distinct pleasure of encouraging one another, to be sure. But we also have the joy of receiving encouragement. Honestly, this is what "speaking the truth in love" (Ephesians 4:15) means. It's reminding people of what they already know. It's giving them a little push to the surface of truth when they need it.

When this need for truth telling would pop up, we'd send each other a text with the red balloon emoji. It was a tiny, virtual SOS signal that we needed some encouragement, some truth spoken into our lives.

When I'd send a red balloon text, it felt humbling because it meant I wasn't able to pull myself out of untruths. However, it was always met with words of truth from someone with a fresher mind about whatever I was dwelling on. And when I got a red balloon text, it was always a joy to grab Jess's hand as we swam to the surface of belief, gulped the fresh air of truth, and floated on top of the deep. We were living out the apostle Paul's charge: "Encourage one another and build each other up, just as in fact you are doing" (1 Thessalonians 5:11).

That resistance, that effort you're putting in to walk in a

different direction, is exactly what seems to create new circuits in your brain.[1] Sometimes you just have to memorize and meditate on the good news loops out of obedience in order to start to make the correct synapses. Memorize it, and then repeat the good news to yourself over and over.

I've realized that the three kinds of false belief—*I can't do this, I'm not enough,* and *nothing is ever going to change*—can all be combatted with one simple addition. When we flip the script and add "with [or in] the Lord," we've got short, memorable truth at the ready.

- "I can do this with the Lord."
- "I'm enough in the Lord."
- "Things will change with the Lord."

The Lord is truly the answer. Memorize whatever version that gives you the truth you need. Write it on your mirror. Put Post-It notes on your cubicle wall. Put it to the tune of your favorite song. You don't need wildly innovative methods, just memorable ones.

Dr. Norman Doidge, a noted psychiatrist and researcher, writes, "Neurons that fire together wire together," and "neurons out of sync fail to link."[2] We want distance between us and the bad news loops, and we want to keep the good news close so it becomes an integral part of the way we think.

There is a modern Western idea that if we just know more, we can be powerful and change more. But I've found that the idea of knowing more doesn't do much if we're not meditating on Scripture and letting it sink deep into our bones. It doesn't change anything to just know the Bible; we must chew on it every day and let it change us. Obedience cements our understanding.

Because we live in a temporal reality—moving through time and earthly circumstances—our minds always need renewing and transforming. Our minds aren't a "one and done" kind of makeover job. We need constant spackling, patching, and sanding. We need the old trails in our minds to grow wild again so our path is blocked. We need to constantly plod over fresh earth and, like a wild woman with a machete, daily tear down the greens that cover our new paths.

Renewing our minds is a little like living in a remote area. We're going to have to go to battle with the land every single day. We're never going to arrive; we're not going to be able to check this off our color-coded to-do list. We're not going to grow up and out of our need to continually do the work. This is a lifestyle kind of process, and we need to get good at this practice.

This is life-and-death work. This is the life and health of your spiritual walk and your mental faithfulness. God gave you a mind, a really lovely mind. It's full of memories you love, and some thoughts that don't bring you joy or God glory. It's time to give them to God to redeem and transform. It's time to let the bad news die, hit the ground, and break open into fresh new thoughts and resurrection truth.

We need resistance to train our minds to be strong. Rather than working against ourselves and becoming exhausted in the process, we need to work against the realities of a fallen world, the powers and the principalities, the lies and the deception. This is more than enough weight to pull and push against.

The Spirit works against the fallen parts of our flesh to mold it and make it more like Jesus. We need to push back against the fallen parts of life, the things that threaten to consume us. We have been given dominion here. We are to train and subdue our flesh, to bring it into the light and under the right authority of God.

So when despair comes, push against it, and your mind will become stronger. When humiliation threatens, remember what it means to be humbled in the Lord. You cannot be found out, because you are found in Him. When you believe that nothing is ever going to change, remind yourself that He has the power to change *everything* and that His power is alive in you through the Holy Spirit.

We don't need to create something new or original here. Scripture already lays out ancient pathways to follow, even though the landscape of our lives looks radically different than the landscapes of those who lived in Bible times. I would argue that this renewing of our minds is even more important today when we see how many things—noise, comparison, etc.—are operating against us. I encourage you to feel grounded in these truths, because there is nothing new here, nothing new under the sun. Scripture offers these tried and true ways to sustain us in our fight against the bad news we tell ourselves—news that is no match for the good news that Jesus offers.

RENEW YOUR MIND

Do not conform to the pattern of this world, but be transformed by the renewing of your mind. Then you will be able to test and approve what God's will is—his good, pleasing and perfect will.

ROMANS 12:2

Instead of letting your mind reflect the state of your day—noisy, rushed, harried, discontented—renew your mind. Keep it fixed on what you know to be true: with Christ you *can* do it;

in Him, you *are* enough; He is powerful enough to bring about change in *any* life or situation. Retune the songs you sing to yourself, and He will change your mind over time. It won't be fast, and it won't feel perfect or steady all the time, but He will make that change.

GRAB HOLD OF YOUR THOUGHTS

> We demolish arguments and every pretension that sets itself up against the knowledge of God, and we take captive every thought to make it obedient to Christ.
>
> 2 CORINTHIANS 10:5

Once you hear and acknowledge your false beliefs, you need to become adept at grabbing them out of the chatter in your mind and holding them up to the truth you know. You flip the script and say it back to yourself. You can't just hear the false beliefs and let them go. The apostle Paul in 2 Corinthians 10:5 challenges us to grab those thoughts and make them obedient to the truth we know. This is another way we can embody truth as we obey it. As we align our thoughts with Christ, our very brains change biologically.

PRAY WITHOUT CEASING

> Do not be anxious about anything, but in every situation, by prayer and petition, with thanksgiving, present your requests to God. And the peace of God, which transcends all understanding, will guard your hearts and your minds in Christ Jesus.

> Finally, brothers and sisters, whatever is true, whatever
> is noble, whatever is right, whatever is pure, whatever is
> lovely, whatever is admirable—if anything is excellent or
> praiseworthy—think about such things.
>
> PHILIPPIANS 4:6–8

We have a protector in the Lord. When we are actively praying throughout the day, we are in tune with the truth that He will guard our minds. He will keep them from running off course, especially when we are thinking about pure, noble, right, true, lovely, and admirable things. This isn't positive thinking in the do-it-yourself, "fake it till ya make it" kind of way, but it's keeping our minds fixed on the beauty of God. When I think of how beautiful my little boy's eyelashes look when he sleeps, it's hard to entertain the thought that I am failing as his mom. When I think about the pure loveliness of a sunrise, it's hard to imagine a world where God doesn't make things new.

Somehow our natural world reflects and reminds us of the spiritual truth of God. When we are constantly beholding the beauty of His world and His people, it is difficult to also entertain false beliefs.

CONSTANTLY PUT ON YOUR NEW SELF

> You were taught, with regard to your former way of life, to
> put off your old self, which is being corrupted by its deceitful
> desires; to be made new in the attitude of your minds; and to
> put on the new self, created to be like God in true righteous-
> ness and holiness.
>
> EPHESIANS 4:22–24

When I was in high school, even before I actually came to follow Jesus myself, I was in a youth group small group that studied an old book called *The Green Letters*. The book was not light reading by any means, but the archaism of the language helped it stick somehow. The author, Miles Stanford, wrote letters to other believers, and when collected, they became a little primer of the Christian faith.

Stanford wrote a lot about the new self and the old self. It was confusing to me as a fifteen-year-old, for whom the idea of an old self would have been new. However, after weeks of studying, I began to see more clearly the idea of an old self. We need to keep putting off the part of us that is apart from God. We need to keep taking off the part of us that is set on our own ways. In this, we are made new in the attitudes of our minds.

So we need to humble ourselves every day, submit ourselves to God, repent of our wayward independence, and decide again to throw off the part of ourselves that desires its own way. The fruit from that pursuit, the pursuit of being clothed only with Christ, will be a renewed mind.

SET YOUR MIND ON THINGS ABOVE

> Set your minds on things above, not on earthly things. For you died, and your life is now hidden with Christ in God. When Christ, who is your life, appears, then you also will appear with him in glory.
>
> COLOSSIANS 3:2–4

It can be easy to think that this verse is simply reminding us to not think about sinful things. However, I believe Paul is also imploring us to take our eyes off our perceived earthly limitations. When we believe that we can't, we aren't, and we won't ever be, we are disbelieving the very truth about God. God says in Jesus we can and in Him we are, and it is only in Him that we have hope for all that will be.

STAY ON THE PATH

> Stay on the path that the Lord your God has commanded you to follow. Then you will live long and prosperous lives in the land you are about to enter and occupy.
>
> DEUTERONOMY 5:33 NLT

This is perhaps the most difficult instruction of all. I am a fan of projects, and fits and spurts and never-ending propositions stress me out. But the way of God is a steady faithfulness on one path. This path is narrow, but it promises abundance. This is the part that takes lifelong steadfastness. We need to stay on the right paths we make in our minds. When God rewires our understanding, we need to stand firm and refuse to go back to the old and easy ways. If we stay on the path God has commanded us to follow, we will see His fruits.

This treading of the new paths is faithfulness in the moment. It's faithfulness to do hard things. It's faithfulness to believe this work is beneficial. You can do this. You were made for this. You renew your mind, and God will transform you.

You renew; He transforms. The pressure is off when it comes to the results. It may not look like you expected, and it may not be immediate. But the changes will be there. You just need to do the daily hard work of walking down the path you know is right and true. It is only this daily faithfulness that will leave you with a mind and a heart you didn't know was possible—through your work and with God's strength.

PART FOUR

Wholehearted and Single-Minded Living

CHAPTER THIRTEEN

More and More Like Christ at Every Turn

All human nature vigorously resists grace because grace changes us and the change is painful.

FLANNERY O'CONNOR,
THE HABIT OF BEING

*A*s the apostle Paul tells us in Romans 12:2, we renew and God transforms. This means you are a changed woman when you renew your mind. God makes us different than we were before. How great is our God! Life change is the stuff of full-out "praise hands." It doesn't mean everything is automatically perfect or that it will always feel good. It doesn't mean we'll never tread the familiar paths of false belief again. But God made our minds to grow and renew as we take our thoughts captive and walk down new mental paths. How creative, how personal, how intimate of God that He would want to make us new as we change our minds!

Where you were once frantic, you're now peaceful. Where you were once confused and conflicted, you are now rightly aligned. Where you were once frustrated, you are now contented and satisfied. Where you were once despondent, you are now full of joy. Where you once felt incapable, you now know that God is more than able.

This is the classic "before and after" kind of picture. It's split down the center, with a dividing line marking what *was* from what *is*. You were inhabiting false beliefs, maybe unintentionally disbelieving our very good God; now you're walking in the light of embodying and obeying real truth in the real world. This is the nature of being a new creation. We get to point at God and how good He is for changing us that one time.

But the reality is, we're being made new *all the time*. This is what God does. This is what God promises when He asks us to—when He commands us to—renew our minds. He promises to transform us, to change us into something entirely new. This is good, because we certainly can't transform ourselves any more than a larva can strive and struggle to become a butterfly.

The reality is that we never "arrive." We will continue to trip up, to take one step forward and two steps back. But we place our hope in the God who never fails to meet us where we are, the God who continually makes us new.

What happens in that impossibly narrow divide between before and after is actually a hefty amount of soul work. It takes recognition, surrender, repentance, and obedience. What happens in that middle space demands we lay down the very contents of our minds for examination.

That middle space, that narrow line in the picture, is where the work is done. It is where you lay yourself out on the Great Physician's table and tell Him where it hurts. He asks you how your health has been. Have you been taking your thoughts captive? Have you been walking the road of obedience? Have you been returning like a dog to its vomit or a fool to their folly?

The narrowness of that middle line in the picture of the before and after is a mercy, I think. By the time we're in the "after" phase, that line has shrunk down to be barely visible when we look at the photo. Before you were *this*, and now you are *that*. Life was hard, and now it's better. It's not perfect, but it's better. If we had to remember every excruciating moment of being brought low and then restored, we'd think twice before we would ever submit to it again.

It's imperative to submit to it over and over, hour by hour, doing whatever it takes. The work of renewing our minds begins again every morning. Thank God that His mercies are new every morning to meet us in this challenge. This is a daily kind of task, a liturgy. We can build our life with God around this rhythm. We renew our minds, making them more aligned with Him, and He transforms us to the very likeness of Christ.

This is good, practical news. He is making us new over and over. Even though we acquire false beliefs and years of neural pathway growth that aren't serving us or the Lord, He is good to keep transforming us. He painstakingly removes the buildup the world has left, as though we are His only child.

This renewing of our minds can be a place we learn to obey. This submission to His work is not always comfortable. But God will ask us to do hard things, and we can use these hard things as a purifying, refining obedience.

I learned an important lesson in cleaning and restoration while surrounded by priceless works of art on ancient cobblestone streets. When I was in college, I spent a summer studying art history in Florence, Italy. The narrow streets that were created for foot traffic and the occasional chariot now were thick with exhaust from the ridiculous horde of tiny cars and motorbikes. The ancient buildings were still standing, but what had been built for an empire now housed 7-Eleven-type convenience stores. As an American, I think anything with a two-hundred-year history is awe-inspiring, but the building I took classes in had been standing for closer to one thousand years. And I stayed in a glorious little hotel called Hotel California, of all things.

I traveled all over Italy and saw some of the most beautiful religious imagery ever created. The piece I remember being absolutely amazed by was Michelangelo's *Pietà*, which is housed in St. Peter's Basilica in Rome. *Pietà* means "pity" in English, and it's a sculpture of Mary holding Jesus, who had just been taken off the cross. Michelangelo is only one of many of his contemporaries to paint and sculpt this scene. But his is work of art is otherworldly magnificent.

Mary is holding Jesus across her lap like she must have when He was a sleeping toddler and all gangly arms and legs in her arms. Michelangelo was so adept at sculpting that you could see the pressure of Mary's fingers clutching Jesus' back as she held His weight. I wish I could have stayed longer to look at every fold of her dress and every rib down Jesus' side. Something about seeing Jesus and His mother, Mary, in such an intimate, last embrace has always stayed at the top of my mind.

Most days we had art history class in front of some of the most famous, priceless works of Renaissance art. Professor Duckworth was not a believer, but she was a fanatic about religious art. As we sat in front of a fresco or sculpture, we'd spend hours discussing the minutiae of the work. It became clear to me that everything in the paintings and sculptures had a purpose. The majority of people in the Renaissance era were illiterate, so the church and wealthy patrons commissioned art to tell the biblical story.

A chalice in a painting symbolized the wine at the Last Supper, with the holder of the chalice depicted as set apart or consecrated. A composition formed in the shape of a triangle symbolized the Trinity. Images of Jesus with His thumb, pointer, and middle finger symbolized a blessing, and there are even art pieces of the baby Jesus with His hands in the blessing position.

The gospel writers were symbolized as winged animals. Matthew was a winged human; Mark was a winged lion; Luke was a winged bull; and John was an eagle. The symbolism in this religious art was fascinating to me. After weeks of learning in front of the real pieces that I'd later only study in photographs and slides, I began to be able to discern the larger story the artist was aiming to depict.

I've never gotten over the fact that I lived less than two blocks from where Michelangelo's *David* is housed. Can you believe it? There are people who live in Florence, surrounded by masterful art every day of their lives!

The giant sculpture of the biblical king currently resides in the Galleria dell'Accademia. When I was there, *David* was undergoing a half-million-dollar cleaning project. Scaffolding surrounded the sculpture when I viewed *David*, but the scaffolding only added to the experience.

After such thorough lessons on biblical art symbols, I couldn't help but begin to see symbols in everything. The scaffolding made some sort of symbolic sense to me. I started to have a holy imagination for symbolism by which I could view what God is doing in the world.

The preservationists erected the scaffolding because *David* needed renewing. This was a magnificent work of art that needed to be cared for. In some areas, there were two centuries of wax built up on the sculpture. The Carrara marble was dark gray in places from impurities that were damaging to the rock itself.

But the scaffolding helped the renewers and preservationists reach David. The scaffolding allowed them to renew *David* with care rather than force. The preservationists didn't need to take a hammer to make *David* new. They didn't need to bulldoze him and start over. And this isn't what we're talking about when we think of renewing our minds either. The art preservationists used distilled water brushed over Japanese paper with specialized brushes to restore *David*. It was painstaking and deliberate. It was careful and considered.

And this is the way God transforms us. We can erect scaffolding of good practices, like identifying our false beliefs and taking them captive. And then God acts as the Master Restorer, transforming us into who He made us to be. He gently brushes off the deposits of years of wrong thinking. If we submit, He transforms us, not with a bulldozer or through demolition, but by careful, deliberate pressure. When we take every opportunity to renew our minds, His pressure is like a light brushstroke that adds up over time. He makes us new a million little times. His work is painstaking and deliberate. It is careful and considered.

We choose to cling to God for our hope, our strength, and our provision. Because these things are hard and it's difficult to live lives of faithfulness, we learn the deep lessons of our faith. We learn the mysteries of God because we are forced to draw close to Him. We learn to abide because we're left with no other choice.

We can use every thought, every occasion we change our minds, to move us closer to the Lord. Every lesson, every trial, every errant motive, can be brought to Him and can be used by Him to make us more like Christ. As we grow to be more Christlike throughout our lifetimes, we will eventually begin to take on some of His unshakable ways.

When we renew our minds and allow God to transform us, we experience growth in our walk with the Lord. We begin to feel less stale and lifeless. We no longer carry the heavy burden of frustration from trying hard and failing because we're trying hard in our own strength.

For me, I no longer had to put on a well-intentioned performance. I didn't need to *act* like I was growing, because I really had started growing again. My stale faith was fresh again. It was like I was experiencing the joy of my salvation anew.

We don't have to keep fighting the same old things. When we become new, we're not bogged down by the same old bad news we've always dwelt on. We're able to get going on new paths of growth. We pull the weeds, prune the dead branches, and leave energy for our roots to dive deeper.

When our hearts are made whole by the renewing of our minds, we are more aware of what God is doing in the world. We have spiritual eyes to see Him at work, and we're ready to serve.

Before our friend Lainey and her husband were matched with a foster child, some friends were at her house one night painting the nursery. Lainey wanted the baby who would lie in that crib to know that she was just as wanted as Lainey's biological children. She wanted her to know she was loved beyond imagination by a God who is bigger than comprehension. She wanted her to sense that she is loved by the same God, no matter whether she is with her biological mom or with Lainey as her stand-in mama.

Lainey hung lyrics to the worship song "Oceans (Where Feet May Fail)" above the crib, indicating the deep faith this obedience was demanding. This is what it looks like to live with an undivided heart. Even when our beliefs call us to do difficult things, we do them in obedience, because being a wholehearted believer who follows closely after God is His best for us.

Lainey's heart is knit together so tightly that all of it is surrendered to God. I've known her since before she knew Jesus. In those "Before Christ" days, she was always looking to pick a fight. She knew the world could be harsh beyond words, and she was going to make sure you knew she could defend herself. She was sassy—and not in a cute way. She had a hard edge that defied easy explanation. But I'm telling you that God swept her right up into His grand story, and she takes everything God says through

Scripture or the Spirit at face value. She hears, and then she obeys. Lainey is walking without an integrity gap. She knows who she is in the Lord, and she lives a congruent life.

Over the course of the last year, Lainey had begun to sense that God was giving her an opportunity to obey by taking in a child from the state foster care system. This opportunity led, though, to quite a struggle. She felt the battle rage between her flesh and her spirit. Her "old self" reared up, because fostering a child flew in the face of everything she wanted for her life. She already had two kids she adored. She worked full-time as an ultrasound tech at a hospital. And she was discipling more than fifteen women as an expression of her service to the church and to the Lord.

She has admitted to having a Type A personality, and before she became a Christ follower, she was tightly wound, with a high need for control. Foster care was certainly destined to be upsetting to her life plan. However, she couldn't shake the call of God to obey. She sensed it was less about the actual fostering and more about following God wherever He was leading her. This was a big act of obedience.

I remember Lainey telling me that God had done so much for her, having changed her whole life, that she couldn't imagine how she could deny Him this obedience. She knew what it meant to obey, but her flesh was struggling to give up control. Yet because Lainey has built a scaffolding of good practices, she is allowing God to transform her every day. She's always renewing her mind with truth, and she is allowing the wrestling to make her more like Christ.

She and her husband are now the foster parents of an eleven-month-old girl from a neighboring town. Lainey asked God to break her heart in the way His heart is broken for people, and she tells me that she wept for weeks when her foster daughter came to stay. She wasn't weeping for herself—for the difficulty this brought to their lives—but for the brokenness that families are experiencing all over the world. She knows that her heart is being made more whole through its breaking. God is sewing it together.

Change is not comfortable, and obedience never comes without change. But when we obey, our integrity gap closes even further, and we are transformed to become more like Christ. When the change and renewing are slow or difficult, we don't despair, because we see the power of God at work in our lives. We see Him making us more and more like Christ at every turn. I think it's important to note that not a single part of our relationship with God is about the outcome; it is all about the process. If we did right things with a wrong heart, that right thing might actually be wrong.

I am notoriously terrible about celebrating small victories, but my friend Sara celebrates everything. She celebrates the beginning of summer break. She celebrates the Kentucky Derby. Sara even celebrates the opening ceremony of the Olympics with internation-ally themed food that has tiny flags inserted in it with toothpicks. I want to be more like my friend Sara and throw a party every time I recognize that I've been made more like Jesus. Is there anything worthier of celebration?

Even when we're slow to change or we experience a setback—and we will—we can trust that God will uphold His end of the bargain. We may not feel the change, but it's happening. Every single change of our minds when God is transforming it brings Him glory. And we're the ones who get a front-row seat to that glory. We get to see and believe another facet of His goodness when we are transformed.

CHAPTER FOURTEEN

We Finally Get Out of Our Own Way

Not I, not any one else can travel that road for you,
You must travel it for yourself.

It is not far, it is within reach.
Perhaps you have been on it since you were born and
     did not know.

> WALT WHITMAN,
> "SONG OF MYSELF"

*I*n Jesus' time on earth, He often spoke in parables, or bite-size stories, to get His points across. One of my favorites is the parable of the sower, found in Matthew 13:

> That same day Jesus went out of the house and sat by the lake. Such large crowds gathered around him that he got into a boat and sat in it, while all the people stood on the shore. Then he told them many things in parables, saying: "A farmer went out to sow his seed. As he was scattering the seed, some fell along the path, and the birds came and ate it up. Some fell on rocky places, where it did not have much soil. It sprang up quickly, because the soil was shallow. But when the sun came up, the plants were scorched, and they withered because they had no root. Other seed fell among thorns, which grew up and choked the plants. Still other seed fell on good soil, where it produced a crop—a hundred, sixty or thirty times what was sown. Whoever has ears, let them hear."
>
> The disciples came to him and asked, "Why do you speak to the people in parables?"
>
> He replied, "Because the knowledge of the secrets of the kingdom of heaven has been given to you, but not to them. Whoever has will be given more, and they will have an abundance."

Let's stop here, in the middle of the parable, where the disciples ask Jesus why in the world He always tells them stories. So in verse 13, Jesus says this:

"This is why I speak to them in parables:

"Though seeing, they do not see;
though hearing, they do not hear or understand."

Matthew 13:14–15 is a fulfillment of Isaiah 6:9–10:

"You will be ever hearing but never understanding;
you will be ever seeing but never perceiving.
For this people's heart has become calloused;
they hardly hear with their ears,
and they have closed their eyes.
Otherwise they might see with their eyes,
hear with their ears,
understand with their hearts
and turn, and I would heal them."

I like to think I'd believe Jesus if He was standing in front of me. If He was kneeling and scratching a lesson in the Jerusalem dirt, I hope my heart would be turned toward His. But these words from Isaiah make me wonder.

These words tell me that people's hearts are calloused. They are hardly listening with their ears. They're not even looking for what God is doing, because they've closed their eyes.

I'm afraid this is what happens when we live with divided hearts. In fact, I'm sure of it because the Bible is clear about the effects of a heart that doesn't fully love God. When we don't truly believe what we say we believe, we end up hardened and unmoving. We don't yield to anything the Lord is doing. We're not even paying attention.

In this passage from Isaiah, he goes on to say that if we will open our eyes and listen closely, if we truly understand—not just hear but understand—with our hearts, He will heal us.

Let's finish up the parable, because Jesus tells the best stories.

> "But blessed are your eyes because they see, and your ears because they hear. For truly I tell you, many prophets and righteous people longed to see what you see but did not see it, and to hear what you hear but did not hear it.
>
> "Listen then to what the parable of the sower means: When anyone hears the message about the kingdom and does not understand it, the evil one comes and snatches away what was sown in their heart. This is the seed sown along the path. The seed falling on rocky ground refers to someone who hears the word and at once receives it with joy. But since they have no root, they last only a short time. When trouble or persecution comes because of the word, they quickly fall away. The seed falling among the thorns refers to someone who hears the word, but the worries of this life and the deceitfulness of wealth choke the word, making it unfruitful. But the seed falling on good soil refers to someone who hears the word and understands it. This is the one who produces a crop, yielding a hundred, sixty or thirty times what was sown."

If you've heard the good news, the message of God's kingdom, but don't understand it at all, Satan snatched it up before it had a chance to take root. Jesus' parable says the seed was sown along the path, which means it was out in the open, unprotected, and probably not cared for. A path has hard soil, trodden down, easy to travel.

If you've heard the good news and received it with joy but then it fizzled out, it might be because the root did not grow deeply enough. It didn't have strength and fortitude when conditions were not favorable. Remember that we need to hear the good news over and over. We need to accept the gospel every day for a multitude of shortcomings. When you receive the news with joy, but it doesn't sink down into your heart, look at how deep you're letting the root grow. Are you faithfully taking the good news and allowing it to change you? Are you applying it to your thoughts and renewing your mind with truth?

If you've heard the good news but haven't been bearing fruit, check to see if the worries of life or the trappings of comfort and security have gotten the best of you. Are you distracted? Is the noise of life or your tendency to make comparisons in relationships making it difficult to hear? The thorns in life are real. They're present, and they're not always immediately painful. Sometimes the proverbial thorns lull us into thinking we're safe when, in reality, our zest for life and our ability to be spiritually awake and sensitive are being squeezed out of us.

If you cultivate the good soil of your mind and heart, you will hear the good news and understand it deep in your bones (increasingly over the course of a lifetime), and your life will bear fruit—the lifelong kind of fruit that comes from faithfully hearing God's word and taking it to heart, making sure to submit your false beliefs to His power to change. It's not the kind of fruit that looks fancy and then spoils. It's the fruit that ripens in season—only because we're connected to Jesus.

Jesus says the seed that falls on good soil will produce a crop. It will yield either a hundred, sixty, or thirty times what was sown. Jesus isn't guaranteeing your life will be wildly successful by the world's standards. This Scripture passage is not telling you your life will be full of comfort or ease. But it is saying that if you renew your mind, God will transform you and your life will bear much fruit.

The women who have most impacted me are those who aren't stuck in their own heads; they are women who live out for themselves the truths they preach to others. Oh, how I want to be that kind of woman all the time! I want to be done with the exhaustion of a busy, messy mind. I want the good news that I know to be true to permeate my entire being, so much so that my spirit outweighs my flesh. I want to embody the truth I know, to walk it out of my head and into my life.

Once we get out of our own heads, we get out of our own way.

I wish I could tell you the battle ends here for you. I wish I could tell you you'll get to be in the cheering section from here on out. I wish that was true for me too. I always seem to be hoping to grow out of my need for the Lord. Something in my "old self" keeps whispering that I'd be more special or impressive if I didn't need Jesus. I sometimes think I'd give anything to have a placid, perfected mind.

However, that's not the way God has wired us. And it's not His best for us. The only way to a renewed, transformed mind is the power of Christ. Our brains are always creating new connections, which means we're always going to be needing to renew our minds, to make sure those connections are good ones. And when God asks us to renew our minds, He gives us a promise in return. He promises to transform us.

The only times the powerful Greek word *metamorphoō* (translated as "transfigure" or "transform") is used in the Bible are in two of the gospel accounts of the transfiguration of Christ (Matthew 17:2; Mark 9:2) and in two of Paul's letters (Romans 12:2; 2 Corinthians 3:18).

When we renew our minds, we submit ourselves to a holistic change, a renovation. When we are changed by the power of God Himself, we are changed from the inside out. W. E. Vine describes the meaning of *metamorphoō* like this:

> *Metamorphoō* ... is used in the passive voice ... of believers, Rom 12:2, "be ye transformed," the obligation being to undergo a complete change which, under the power of God, will find expression in character and conduct; *morphō* lays stress on the inward change, *schēma* (see the preceding verb in that verse, *suschēmatizō*) lays stress on the outward ... The present continuous tenses indicate a process; 2 Cor 3:18 describes believers as being "transformed (RV) into the same image" (i.e., of Christ in all His moral excellencies), the change being effected by the Holy Spirit.[1]

This is the kind of transforming act God will do on your mind when you renew it. As Mark tells us in his account of Jesus' transfiguration, *you can become radiant.*

> And [Jesus] said to them, "Truly, I say to you, there are some standing here who will not taste death until they see the kingdom of God after it has come with power."
> And after six days Jesus took with him Peter and James and John, and led them up a high mountain by themselves.

> And he was transfigured before them, and his clothes became radiant, intensely white, as no one on earth could bleach them.
>
> MARK 9:1–3 ESV

It's late—long after dinner has ended—and the sky has grown dim. Starlight pricks the black sky. The group of men have left the upper room and have been walking for a while. Walking with Jesus means you never know exactly where you're going; you just know you're following Jesus. But the disciples have gotten used to this, since they've been following Him for years now. The men are all talking as they walk, even though the mood has grown somber. Peter is kicking rocks on the path, wondering why his best friend is doubting his love. Peter keeps his head down. Is it out of shame? Frustration? Even Peter can't tell.

Peter sees the Mount of Olives looming in the distance. The mountain is like a shadow swimming in the deep dark late into the night. The group edges up to the gates of a garden; they've arrived at Gethsemane. They've been there before—it's one of their places to hang out. Jesus invites the eleven men into the garden—Judas is absent since the betrayal. The gate swings open for everyone to enter. "Come and follow me," Jesus says, for what must feel like the millionth time. It's always an invitation with Jesus.

The gate closes, and the eleven men follow Jesus in. The paths are lined with twisty olive trees, and that same twistiness vibrates among the men. No one knows exactly what Jesus will do next. No one ever knows exactly.

"Sit here while I go over there and pray" (Matthew 26:36). He says this to eight men while grabbing the hands of just three of them—Peter, James, and John. He pulls the three deeper into the garden, away from the other men.

He leans close to these three—His closest friends, the men He had invited into His life over and over again. They'd been to weddings and (almost) funerals together, fished together, and traveled together. He had been showing them how to live, and now Jesus knows it's almost time to show them how to die. Jesus looks troubled. Tears drop like rivers down the dust that covers His face.

This is what Jesus does. He continually reveals more and more of Himself to us as we follow Him deeper in. As we hear, understand, and obey, Jesus invites us into more intimacy with Him.

When Jesus walked this earth, many people knew Him, but He chose only a few to be His disciples, His faithful followers. And of those disciples, it was only Peter, James, and John whom He trusted enough to show how broken and tired He was. Jesus does this with us too. We say we want to "go deeper" with Jesus, and as my pastor says, this usually means we want to know more *about* Jesus. But Jesus doesn't care if we know about Him. The Bible says that even the demons know of Him (Luke 4:41; James 2:19). As we see in this account in Matthew's gospel, depth with Jesus looks like following Him further in.

As a child, I never fully trusted the adults in my life. I generally felt like I knew better than they did, as embarrassing as it is to admit. I *hated* going anywhere without advance notice—without knowing the plan and the reason for going in the first place.

I couldn't wait to become an adult, mostly because then I could eat cake and Kit Kats for breakfast and be the boss of me. Obviously, I had a few things to learn! Especially when it comes to the way of Jesus.

He still asks me to follow Him deeper in, with rarely an explanation of where we're going or why we're doing it in the first place.

The only times I've ever grown closer in relationship with Jesus is when I've followed Him wholeheartedly somewhere new.

Jesus and the three disciples have now gone further in, and He turns to them and says, "My soul is overwhelmed with sorrow to the point of death. Stay here and keep watch with me" (Matthew 26:38). Then He pushes a little farther into the garden between the twisty olive trees and begins to talk with His Dad. Jesus falls on His face and begs the Father to pass Him over. I can imagine the tears streaming down His dust-covered face, telling His Father He'll follow Him deeper still if He asks.

How many times does my commitment to follow Jesus start with what feels like a tiny death? I beg God to pass me over all the time. *Don't ask me to do it. Don't tell me to lay it down.* All the while, Jesus is holding open the garden gate, telling me that His way is life.

How often do I get confused about life and death when it comes to following Jesus? I say I want more of Him, and the only way to get more is to follow Him to death and then to life resurrected. It's not about knowing more *about* Jesus; it's about following Him, about embracing His way in obedience and faith. It's about believing that His footsteps are good and right and that they'll lead to life for me and for others.

This is what Jesus says. He says, "I am the way and the truth and the life" (John 14:6). He is the way to life eternal, but He is also the way to life right now. Holding His hand as we follow Him into the depths of a garden teeming with life, even as it leads us toward a death of sorts, is the way we know Him more. This is the way we go deeper with Jesus. We actually follow Him deeper in His way.

We become more like Jesus, and our lives become more whole and less fractured. We begin to do as our spirit wills rather than as our flesh desires. Our thoughts, beliefs, and actions are all pointed in the same direction—toward the way of Jesus.

When we close the integrity gap between our false beliefs and the real-life, good-news truth, we see profound fruit.

We take new ground rather than just holding the line. This is the fun part of our spiritual life with Jesus. The Bible uses a lot of "battle" verbiage. We battle against our flesh. We battle against unseen spiritual forces.

I think it's apt to say that when you're alive to what the Lord is doing, when you've understood the good news, when you renew your mind, you will grow to a point where you are not just holding a defensive line but are expanding the territory of the kingdom.

You'll no longer just have to draw a circle and defend yourself; you'll be able to grow in new, exciting ways. Think about the disciples, Jesus was always calling them into deeper intimacy with Himself. I think that's what happens with us too. When we hear, understand, and obey one bit He's asked of us, we'll get invited into another bit too.

Our brains are designed to be lazy in a sense. There are so many connections and so much information stored that it needs to function very resourcefully. The brain will always choose the most energy-efficient path of thought; therefore, the brain will always choose the neural pathway that is most established and ingrained.[2]

Children's brains are naturally more pliable and moldable than our adult brains, but when we give up thoughts and beliefs that are not serving us well, our brains can change, mimicking the growth in brain connections that we experience as a child. In a sense, this helps us become more childlike in our brains and in our faith, always being open to new and fresh things from the Lord.

We get to provide spiritual care for others, not just for ourselves. There's a well-known adage that the church is not a retirement home for saints but a hospital for sinners. This word picture breaks down, however, when there are no proverbial doctors or nurses in the building. The church needs Christians who are spiritually mature, who follow faithfully and closely after Christ to do the work of triage and wound care. We need to help nurse back to health the wounded in our ranks.

We get to use the way God has changed us as a testimony to His goodness. Many people find it awkward to strike up spiritual conversations with others who don't share the same beliefs. However, everyone loves a good "before and after" story. We are called to bear witness (to tell the truth to people) to God's goodness in our lives (see Isaiah 43:10; Matthew 5:16; 28:19; Acts 1:8; 22:15; 1 Peter 3:15; and many other passages). The simplest and, surprisingly, most effective way to do this is by saying this simple phrase:

I was _____, and because God changed me, now
I'm _____.

For me, this statement takes on many forms, but all of them are true.

- I was anxious, and because God changed me, now I have peace most of the time.
- I was alone, and because God changed me, now I feel like I'm part of something bigger than myself.
- I was afraid to be silent, and because God changed me, now I can face the quiet.

When God changes your life, you want to tell other people about it. And when you tell other people, it often allows them to open up about their own struggles and spiritual stories.

Once you've been changed by the Lord through the renewing of your mind, it becomes part of your DNA. You're a new creation, and you accept transformation every day. You will have a hard time not being noisy about God's good news in your life.

Imagine this. We get to set the future. It's true. We're at a moment in history when it feels like the Christian culture can go one of two ways. We can either own up to the fact that we've had an integrity gap and learn good theology and practice to change it. Or we can let that gap fester and work under a broken system that will keep us from flourishing.

This is our opportunity. This push-pull we feel in life, this resistance, this difficulty, does not have to be in vain. God built our minds—the biology of our brains—to thrive on taking the frustrations of life and giving them to Him. God has given us everything we need to build up the muscles required to become culture makers and reformers. He is faithful to us, and He is good to do the work of transforming our minds.

With my life, I'm choosing to let God root out the bad news in my life and replace it with the abundance of the good news. I'm letting Him shine the light on the loops of false belief I've got on repeat, and then I'm asking Him to change my mind. I believe He's good to do it—every day, every time I renew my mind. He has created my biology to function in this way, and He has done the same for you.

This is the only way forward for those of us who are weary, frustrated, and despairing over the lack of congruence in our spiritual lives. I see this to be true in individual believers and also in the church as a whole. We need our beliefs to line up with our thoughts and actions, and we need this kind of unity in ourselves before we'll ever have unity or power in the world.

The good news we can keep preaching to ourselves is that God is good to do this and to do even more. He is infinitely good to us forevermore. Let it be so.

Imagine your life one year from today. You've lived and grown through all four seasons. You cozied in during the dark, dismal, seemingly dead months of winter, doing the shadowy and quiet and tiring work of examining your mind for the false beliefs that live there. You separated the dark from the light, and as the Lord does, you called what you saw by name, thereby shining the light on your false beliefs.

Then you sat in a brighter light and felt the warmth of spring on your face. You were able to see what was growing in your life—what was a lovely flower and what was a weed. You spent the energy and the labor to pluck the weeds of false belief out of the ground at the root. You were doing the necessary work to keep those false beliefs from growing too deeply and too wide, to keep them from spreading through your whole life.

In the summer, you experienced the fresh revival of a transformed mind. It wasn't perfect every day, but you weren't the same person you were last summer. You took new ground with renewed energy. You experienced that summer feeling where you see your neighbors for the first time in months, because you weren't focused on the inside of your own proverbial house. What a joy it was to see people and serve them rather than to always be so inwardly focused!

And in the autumn, your life put on an unreal display of God's goodness. Fall shows us that things can change. You got to testify that God changed your mind. You once were *that* (hopeless, exhausted, frustrated, defeated), and now you are *this* (filled with joy and peace and hope, looking expectantly to the future). What a picture of God's great love for us!

We have the very mind of Christ, and He sees beyond how things are to how things could be. Imagine what your life will look like after a year of taking your thoughts captive and renewing your mind. It won't be perfect. It will still require daily work, but maybe that daily work will be on a *new* false belief rather than on the one going through your head right now.

He is mighty in you, and He has the power to change your mind. You are mighty because He is in you and you are His handiwork—the masterpiece He's not finished with yet. Allow your mind to be beautifully renewed, and get on with your mission of renewing the world around you with increasing peace, joy, and hope.

Acknowledgments

This book tested my mettle. For some reason, as a Christian writer, I've found that when I commit my heart to a project, I will be challenged by its contents. I must prove that I will practice what I preach, that I will walk the walk I talk so easily about. When the book hits the shelves, I need to be able to stand by what I wrote with my whole self.

To get to that point in a book like this was at times embarrassing and messy. Some days I just couldn't get over the loop of bad news in my head: *I can't do this*. But a bunch of my people told me the truth until I learned to tell myself the truth for long enough to really begin to embody the good news that I *could* partner with the Lord to finish this book. He set forth this good work for me to do long, long ago and now all I had to do was walk hand in hand with Him to its completion.

Mike, my ever-kind, long-suffering husband, thank you. You listen to me rock tumble my ideas until they're polished and pretty.

Boys, thank you for always being on my team. You make mothering a joy. You can do hard things. Thanks for reminding me through your courage that I can do hard things too.

Stephanie, Jenni, and Alicia, you are my book dream team. I wish every author could be so lucky.

The pastors at Genesis Church, you're the best. I'm grateful for your humble leadership and nearness to the Lord.

Barb, your friendship is a gift, and knowing that my boys are always in good hands with you makes it easy to do my job.

Lexi, thanks a zillion that you put up with me every day in the office. Sharing the days with you has been a treat.

Annie, thanks for pulling more weight during the crazy times of writing! I know it's not easy, but you do it with grace and kindness.

Brittney, Whitney, and Lindsey, thanks for being safe friends to work out the faith with.

Jill and Jen, you can't make old friends. Thanks for being those kinds of friends for me.

Jess, thanks for pacing with me after Jesus. You make book writing ten times more fun.

Mom and Brad, glad to look like and love you guys. There's something magical about family. Maddie, welcome to the mix.

Morgan family, thanks for being the kind of family people dream about marrying into.

Grandpa, thanks for hanging out with the boys whenever deadlines got close (and a zillion other times too!). I'm glad we moved back home and can live down the road.

These sure are the good old days.

Real Truths for Bad News Loops

*F*rom a survey of five hundred women from all walks of life, I gleaned the most prevalent bits of "bad news" we tell ourselves every day. You may see some familiar thoughts reflected here. With every bit of bad news, I've countered it with the truth of what God thinks as shown in Scripture. You can also use this as a template to talk back with truth as you uncover the bad news loops you tell yourself.

You think: I am a failure.
God says: I lift those who have fallen.

> [The Lord] helps those who are in trouble; he lifts those who have fallen.
>
> PSALM 145:14 GNT

You think: I can't do this.
God says: Walk by the Spirit, and you can do what I need you to do.

> Walk by the Spirit, and you will not gratify the desires of the flesh.

GALATIANS 5:16

You think: I'm never going to succeed.
God says: Anything and everything is rubbish compared to knowing my Son, Jesus. If you know Jesus intimately, you are a success in my eyes.

> I consider everything a loss because of the surpassing worth of knowing Christ Jesus my Lord, for whose sake I have lost all things. I consider them garbage, that I may gain Christ and be found in him . . . I want to know Christ—yes, to know the power of his resurrection and participation in his sufferings, becoming like him in his death, and so, somehow, attaining to the resurrection from the dead.

PHILIPPIANS 3:8–11

You think: I'm not smart enough.
God says: I don't need you to be smart; I need you to be faithful.

> I did not come with eloquence or human wisdom as I proclaimed to you the testimony about God. For I resolved to know nothing while I was with you except Jesus Christ and him crucified. I came to you in weakness with great fear and trembling. My message and my preaching were not with wise and persuasive words, but with a demonstration of the Spirit's power, so that your faith might not rest on human wisdom, but on God's power.

1 CORINTHIANS 2:1–5

You think: I'm too tired.
God says: I will give you strength and power.

> [The LORD] gives strength to the weary and increases the power of the weak.
>
> ISAIAH 40:29

You think: This is too hard.
God says: Nothing is too hard for me. And I am with you.

> Is anything too hard for the LORD?
>
> GENESIS 18:14

You think: I can't handle this.
God says: You may not be able to handle this situation, but I am enough for you.

> My flesh and my heart may fail,
>> but God is the strength of my heart
>> and my portion forever.
>
> PSALM 73:26

You think: I'm a mess.
God says: I don't look down on you. You will not be put to shame.

> There is now no condemnation for those who are in Christ Jesus.
>
> ROMANS 8:1

You think: I'm not measuring up.

God says: This is not surprising to me, for no one ever has measured up. My goodness is not dependent on your ability.

> All have sinned and fall short of the glory of God.
>
> ROMANS 3:23

You think: Others have it easier because they're more "blessed."
God says: Any kind of suffering in your life—and there will be suffering because this world is broken—I will use for your good. I promise.

> We also glory in our sufferings, because we know that suffering produces perseverance; perseverance, character; and character, hope. And hope does not put us to shame, because God's love has been poured out into our hearts through the Holy Spirit, who has been given to us.
>
> ROMANS 5:3–5

You think: I'm so weak.
God says: That is okay with me. I am mighty in you.

> I will boast all the more gladly about my weaknesses, so that Christ's power may rest on me. That is why, for Christ's sake, I delight in weaknesses, in insults, in hardships, in persecutions, in difficulties. For when I am weak, then I am strong.
>
> 2 CORINTHIANS 12:9–10

You think: No one cares about me.
God says: I know every little hair on your head. I picked your birthday. I love you, and you are not alone.

The very hairs of your head are all numbered. Don't be afraid; you are worth more than many sparrows.

LUKE 12:7

You think: I will always struggle.
God says: I'm working things out, and I won't leave you this way.

He who began a good work in you will carry it on to completion until the day of Christ Jesus.

PHILIPPIANS 1:6

You think: I will never change.
God says: I have already changed you. You are fundamentally different now. And I have not stopped making things new in your life.

If anyone is in Christ, the new creation has come: The old has gone, the new is here!

2 CORINTHIANS 5:17

You think: God can't use me.
God says: I am working in you every day.

God is working in you, giving you the desire and the power to do what pleases him.

PHILIPPIANS 2:13 NLT

You think: I'm done. I give up.
God says: Don't you dare stop now. I am with you, and I will help you.

> God is in the midst of her; she shall not be moved;
> God will help her when morning dawns.
>
> PSALM 46:5 ESV

Notes

Chapter 2: The Bad News Is on Repeat

1. "The Devil in Me," *This American Life*, transcript 340, *NPR*, www
.thisamericanlife.org/340/transcript.
2. Seth J. Gillihan, "What Makes Us Think Such Negative Things
about Ourselves," www.psychologytoday.com/us/blog/think-act-be/
201802/what-makes-us-think-such-negative-things-about-ourselves,
italics original.
3. "The Devil in Me."

Chapter 3: A Look inside Our Heads

1. Luke Dittrich, *Patient H.M.: A Story of Memory, Madness, and
Family Secrets* (New York: Random House, 2016).
2. "Lobotomy," *Oxford Dictionaries*, https://en.oxforddictionaries.com/
definition/lobotomy.
3. Ed Yong, "A Book about Neuroscience's Most Famous Patient
Sparks Controversy," *The Atlantic*, August 12, 2016, www.the
atlantic.com/science/archive/2016/08/the-dark-story-of-neuro
sciences-most-famous-patient/494939.
4. Gregory Boyd and Al Larson, *Escaping the Matrix: Setting Your
Mind Free to Experience Real Life in Christ* (Grand Rapids: Baker,
2005), 31.

5. Karen Ravn, "Some Amazing Facts about Your Unbelievable Brain," *Los Angeles Times*, May 18, 2017, www.latimes.com/health/la-he-hl-brain-facts-20170518-htmlstory.html

6. "Draw Your Nervous System," American Museum of Natural History, www.amnh.org/exhibitions/brain-the-inside-story/brain-promos/for-educators/draw-your-nervous-system.

7. Eric Haseltine, "Five Weird Facts about the Brain You Didn't Know," *Psychology Today*, September 21, 2015, www.psychologytoday.com/us/blog/long-fuse-big-bang/201509/five-weird-facts-about-the-brain-you-didnt-know.

8. Daniel J. Siegel, *The Mindful Brain: Reflection and Attunement in the Cultivation of Well-Being* (New York: Norton, 2007), 29–30.

9. Siegel, *Mindful Brain*, 29.

10. Siegel, *Mindful Brain*, 30.

11. Siegel, *Mindful Brain*, 30.

12. Siegel, *Mindful Brain*, 5.

13. See Charles John Ellicott, "Commentary on Psalms 42:7," *Ellicott's Commentary for English Readers*, www.studylight.org/commentary/psalms/42-7.html.

14. See Albert Barnes, "Commentary on Psalms 42:7," *Barnes Notes on the New Testament*, www.studylight.org/commentary/psalms/42-7.html.

Chapter 4: Our World Is So Noisy

1. "Why Is Everyone So Busy?" *The Economist*, December 20, 2014, www.economist.com/christmas-specials/2014/12/20/why-is-everyone-so-busy.

2. Jennie Allen, "Give Up Trying to Measure Up," *Desiring God*, September 26, 2017, www.desiringgod.org/articles/give-up-trying-to-measure-up.

3. Gregg Easterbrook, "The Nation: Wages of Wealth; All This Progress Is Killing Us, Bite by Bite," *New York Times*, March 14, 2004, www.nytimes.com/2004/03/14/weekinreview/the-nation-wages-of-wealth-all-this-progress-is-killing-us-bite-by-bite.html.

4. Jeff Bullas, "35 Mind Numbing YouTube Facts, Figures and Statistics—Infographic," www.jeffbullas.com/35-mind-numbing -youtube-facts-figures-and-statistics-infographic/.

5. David Grossman, "How Do NASA's Apollo Computers Stack Up to an iPhone?" *Popular Mechanics*, March 13, 2017, www.popular mechanics.com/space/moon-mars/a25655/nasa-computer-iphone -comparison.

6. Grossman, "How Do NASA's Apollo Computers Stack Up to an iPhone?"

7. Martin Doyle, "What Is the Difference between Data and Information?" DQ Global, May 27, 2014, www.dqglobal.com/ 2014/05/27/what-is-the-difference-between-data-and-information.

8. See Nikhil Sharma, "The Origin of Data Information Knowledge Wisdom (DIKW) Hierarchy," www.researchgate.net/publication/ 292335202_The_Origin_of_Data_Information_Knowledge _Wisdom_DIKW_Hierarchy.

9. "10 Key Marketing Trends for 2017 and Ideas for Exceeding Customer Expectations," *IBM Marketing Cloud*, July 19, 2017, https://public.dhe.ibm.com/common/ssi/ecm/wr/en/wrl12345usen/ watson-customer-engagement-watson-marketing-wr-other-papers -and-reports-wrl12345usen-20170719.pdf.

10. Peter Kreeft, *Christianity for Modern Pagans: Pascal's Pensées Edited, Outlined, and Explained* (San Francisco: Ignatius, 1993), 167.

11. Kreeft, *Christianity for Modern Pagans*, 168–69.

12. "Yes, I'd Lie to You," *The Economist*, September 10, 2016, www .economist.com/briefing/2016/09/10/yes-id-lie-to-you.

13. "Number of Social Network Users Worldwide from 2010 to 2021," The Statistics Portal, www.statista.com/statistics/278414/number -of-worldwide-social-network-users.

14. See Brigid Schulte, *Overwhelmed: How to Work, Love, and Play When No One Has the Time* (New York: Farrar, Straus and Giroux, 2015), 43–44.

15. Tim Kreider, "The 'Busy' Trap," *New York Times*, June 30, 2012, https://opinionator.blogs.nytimes.com/2012/06/30/the-busy-trap.

Chapter 5: We Try to Go It Alone

1. Emily P. Freeman, *Graceful (for young Women): Letting Go of Your Try-Hard Life* (Grand Rapids: Baker, 2012).

Chapter 6: We're Numb and Sleepwalking

1. Walter Brueggemann, *The Prophetic Imagination*, 2nd ed. (Minneapolis: Fortress, 2001).

Chapter 9: God Gives Us a Better Way

1. Daniel J. Siegel, *The Mindful Brain: Reflection and Attunement in the Cultivation of Well-Being* (New York: Norton, 2007), 31.
2. Emily P. Freeman, *Grace for the Good Girl: Letting Go of the Try-Hard Life* (Grand Rapids: Baker, 2011), 32.
3. Freeman, *Grace for the Good Girl*, 191, italics original.
4. Macy Halford, "Writing through Devotion and Darkness," Festival of Faith and Writing, April 12, 2018.
5. See Matthew Henry, *Commentary on 1 Corinthians 2*, www.blue letterbible.org/Comm/mhc/1Cr/1Cr_002.cfm?a=1064016.

Chapter 11: The Good Work of Turning Around

1. Christopher Bergland, "How Do Neuroplasticity and Neurogenesis Rewire Your Brain," *Psychology Today*, February 6, 2017, www.psychologytoday.com/us/blog/the-athletes-way/201702/how-do-neuroplasticity-and-neurogenesis-rewire-your-brain.

Chapter 12: Cutting New Paths and Taking New Ground

1. See Norman Doidge, *The Brain That Changes Itself: Stories of Personal Triumph from the Frontiers of Brain Science* (New York: Penguin, 2007), 173.
2. Doidge, *The Brain That Changes Itself*, 63–64.

Chapter 14: We Finally Get Out of Our Own Way

1. W. E. Vine, *Vine's Complete Expository Dictionary of Old and New Testament Words* (Nashville: Nelson, 1996), 639.

2. See Vivian Giang, "What It Takes to Change Your Brain Patterns after Age 25," *Fast Company*, April 28, 2015, www.fastcompany .com/3045424/what-it-takes-to-change-your-brains-patterns -after-age-25.

Wild and Free

A Hope-Filled Anthem for the Woman Who Feels She Is Both Too Much and Never Enough

Jess Connolly and Hayley Morgan

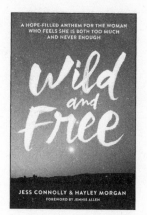

For all the fullness of God available to His daughters, we often feel limited by two defining insecurities: "I am too much," and "I am not enough."

Coauthors and best friends Jess Connolly and Hayley Morgan have felt the same, until one essential question turned the tables on it all: If God is wild and free and he created women, what does this mean for us today?

Wild and Free is an anthem and an invitation in equal parts to find freedom from the cultural captivity that holds us back, and freedom to step into the wild and holy call of God in our lives. With fresh biblical insight tracing all the way back to Eve and a treasury of practical application, Jess and Hayley reveal how women today can walk in the true liberty they already have in Jesus.

Because you don't have to be everything to everyone. You don't have to try so hard to button it up and hold it together. And you certainly don't have to quiet the voice that God gave you when he created you to sing. *Wild and Free* will help you shake off the lies of insecurity in your life and step forward to maximize your God-given influence for his glory and the world's good.

Available in stores and online!

ZONDERVAN®
.com